SPOTLIGHT

D1290868

LOUISVILLE
& THE BOURBON TRAIL

THERESA DOWELL BLACKINTON

Contents

LOUISVILLE &
THE BOURBON TRAIL

LOUISVILLE

Louisville (pronounce it LUH-vul if you want to sound like a local) is where the Fortune 500 meets the nation's largest high school football game, where ostentatious hats go just fine with jeans and t-shirts, and where the country's best Victorian-era preservation district gets along neighborly with striking modern architecture.

Even to those who call it home, Louisville is a conundrum and a contradiction. It consistently sends out reminders that it's not only the biggest city in Kentucky but also the 16th largest in the nation, while at the same time showing itself to be a city of neighborhoods where we're all connected by far less than six degrees of separation. A hint of Midwestern modesty and Northern sensibility seasons the city's personality thanks to its location at the falls of the Ohio River, but Southern hospitality is still the prevailing ingredient. Built on the backs of Irish, German, and other European immigrants as well as enslaved Africans, Louisville has also been influenced by Hispanic culture, as well as the traditions of more recent immigrants and refugees from Eastern Europe and Asia. In a state that paints itself red every election season, Louisville remains a solid dot of blue.

On paper, Louisville might not make sense, but, hey, neither does love, and that's exactly what residents and visitors alike feel for the city. For some, the passion stems from Louisville's big city amenities. The Derby City is home to a performing arts scene that supports one of the nation's most respected theater festivals, so many art galleries as to require

© GREGORY DOWELL

LOUISVILLE

HIGHLIGHTS

◖ **Louisville Slugger Museum & Factory:** Witness the transformation of a piece of ash wood into an iconic Louisville Slugger baseball bat on the factory tour; then relive magical moments in the history of America's pastime in the museum (page 14).

◖ **Muhammad Ali Center:** Going far beyond a simple celebration of the boxing prowess of the self-proclaimed "Greatest" to an exploration of Ali's controversial struggles as well as his great humanitarian acts, this multimedia museum is a must whether you're a boxing fan or not (page 18).

◖ **Old Louisville Tours:** The nation's best preserved Victorian neighborhood, Old

Louisville brims with houses that will make your jaw drop. Take a tour to really dive into the history and architecture of the area, or spend the night in one of the neighborhood's grand B&Bs (page 22).

◖ **Kentucky Derby Museum and Churchill Downs:** Home of the famed Kentucky Derby, Churchill Downs brims with atmosphere as the most historic thoroughbred racetrack in the world, and the adjoining Kentucky Derby Museum lets you experience the thrill of the races even when the track is dark (page 25).

◖ **Louisville Zoo:** An award-winning gorilla exhibit brought the Louisville Zoo to the forefront for animal lovers, but a new-in-2011 arctic animals exhibit as well as the much loved Islands exhibit mean the gorillas have to share the spotlight at this family favorite (page 31).

◖ **First Friday Trolley Hop:** Downtown's Main and Market Streets are home to an ever-expanding population of art galleries, all of which can be explored via trolley on the first Friday of the month, when many galleries host openings, offer snacks and drinks, and make artists available for discourse (page 36).

◖ **Kentucky Derby Festival:** The most exciting two minutes in sports (also known as the Kentucky Derby) cap off not only a day of glamour, madness, and myth at Churchill Downs, but also a two-week party that takes over the entire city and turns Louisville into the place to be in early May (page 37).

◖ **Olmsted Park System:** In a city full of green spaces, the parks designed by Frederick Law Olmsted stand out as hometown favorites. Follow the parkways from the open fields of Cherokee Park to the formal gardens of Shawnee Park to the forested hills of Iroquois Park to experience the system's flagship parks (page 44).

Map of Louisville area showing: INDIANA; Louisville Slugger Museum & Factory; Muhammad Ali Center; First Friday Trolley Hop; Old Louisville Tours; Olmsted Park System; Kentucky Derby Museum and Churchill Downs; Kentucky Derby Festival; Louisville Zoo. Roads: W. MARKET ST, DIXIE HWY, TAYLOR RD, SOUTHSIDE DR, NEW CUT RD, CRITTENDEN DR, PRESTON HWY. Scale: 0 2 mi / 0 2 km. © AVALON TRAVEL

LOOK FOR ◖ TO FIND RECOMMENDED SIGHTS, ACTIVITIES, DINING, AND LODGING.

two monthly trolley hops, research hospitals that perform groundbreaking work like the first hand transplant and first artificial heart transplant, restaurants so good they regularly compete for James Beard awards, and the headquarters of major corporations like Yum! Brands and UPS.

For others, their affection for Louisville relates to its small-town charm and its ability to maintain a strong identity even as the city grows. They love that the first question Louisvillians ask when they meet each other is "Where did you go to high school?", that the city supports its college sports teams with the same gusto as other cities support professional teams, that Heine Brothers is more popular than Starbucks, that downtown's golden-era hotels and Old Louisville's Victorian mansions are as revered as any new development, and that the best museums celebrate local goodness like the Louisville Slugger and Muhammad Ali.

As for what puts Louisville on the world's map, well, it's a little thing really, just a two-minute spectacle. Run every first Saturday in May, the Kentucky Derby and the accompanying two-week festival are the city's pride and joy and the state's largest tourism event. Put it on your calendar, because it's a spectacle that everyone should see at least once.

Whatever your tastes—whether you're a dyed-in-the-cloth city snob or a small-town aficionado—Louisville will win you over. The old dame's no one-hit wonder, and her charm is guaranteed to bring you back time and again.

PLANNING YOUR TIME

Louisville tourism spikes in late April and early May, and for good reason. Many visitors plan their trips around the Kentucky Derby, which is always run on the first Saturday in May, and the Kentucky Derby Festival, which kicks off two weeks before Derby Day. It's a great time to visit. With a little luck, the weather is beautiful, with blue skies, pleasantly warm days, and spring flowers painting the city. With everything spit-polished and shined, the city is prepared to win over the world. But beware, the weather doesn't always cooperate (both snow and unbearable heat have been known to hit on Derby Day), hotel prices will be through the roof (if you can manage to secure a reservation at all), and restaurants will have long waits (show up well before you're hungry).

If you're not set on attending the Derby, choose another time to visit. Over a long weekend, you can cover most of the city's museums and sights all while still enjoying leisurely meals at Louisville's fine restaurants and evenings out on the town. If you're interested in visiting any of the surrounding areas, such as Fort Knox or Shelbyville, tack an extra day onto your itinerary.

Most visitors will want to set themselves up in downtown or Old Louisville, where you'll find the city's best accommodations as well as have easy access to most attractions. If you're looking to explore more of the state, Louisville makes an excellent jumping-off point, with day trips to Lexington, Frankfort, and the Bourbon Trail distilleries easy possibilities.

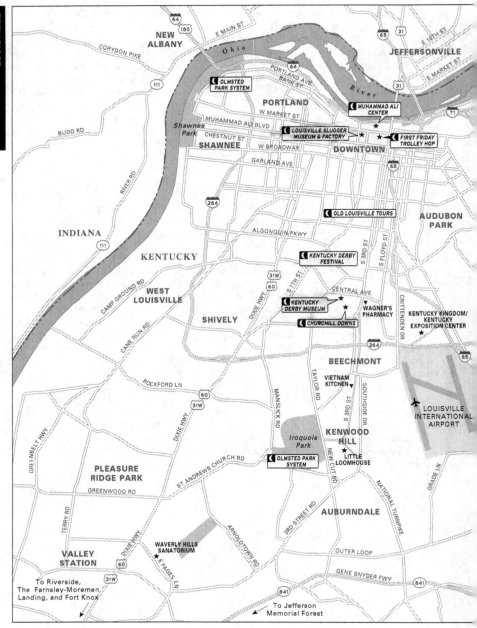

NEW ALBANY

150

54

E MAIN ST

CORYDON PIKE

Ohio

JEFFERSONVILLE

65
31

E 18TH ST

E MARKET ST

31

71

PORTLAND AVE
BANK ST

64

◖ OLMSTED PARK SYSTEM

◖ MUHAMMAD ALI CENTER ★

PORTLAND

W MARKET ST

MUHAMMAD ALI BLVD

Shawnee Park

CHESTNUT ST

SHAWNEE

W BROADWAY

★ ◖ LOUISVILLE SLUGGER MUSEUM & FACTORY

★ ◖ FIRST FRIDAY TROLLEY HOP

DOWNTOWN

BUDD RD

RIVER RD

GARLAND AVE

264

65

◖ OLD LOUISVILLE TOURS

AUDUBON PARK

INDIANA

111

KENTUCKY

ALGONQUIN PKWY

S 3RD ST
S FLOYD ST

◖ KENTUCKY DERBY FESTIVAL

WEST LOUISVILLE

CAMP GROUND RD

31W

S 7TH ST

CENTRAL AVE

SHIVELY

CANE RUN RD

DIXIE HWY

◖ KENTUCKY DERBY MUSEUM ★ ★

★ ▾ WAGNER'S PHARMACY

CRITTENDEN DR

KENTUCKY KINGDOM/ KENTUCKY EXPOSITION CENTER ★

◖ CHURCHILL DOWNS

264

65

BEECHMONT

ROCKFORD LN

60

31W

DIXIE HWY

MANSLICK RD

TAYLOR RD

VIETNAM KITCHEN ▾

S 3RD ST

SOUTHSIDE DR

✈ LOUISVILLE INTERNATIONAL AIRPORT

GREENBELT HWY

PLEASURE RIDGE PARK

GREENWOOD RD

ST ANDREWS CHURCH RD

Iroquois Park

KENWOOD HILL

NEW CUT RD

★ LITTLE LOOMHOUSE

NATIONAL TURNPIKE

GRADE LN

◖ OLMSTED PARK SYSTEM

TERRY RD

AUBURNDALE

3RD STREET RD

ARMOLDTOWN RD

WAVERLY HILLS SANATORIUM ★

E PAGES LN

OUTER LOOP

VALLEY STATION

60

31W

DIXIE HWY

GENE SNYDER FWY

841

841

To Riverside, The Farnsley-Moremen Landing, and Fort Knox

To Jefferson Memorial Forest

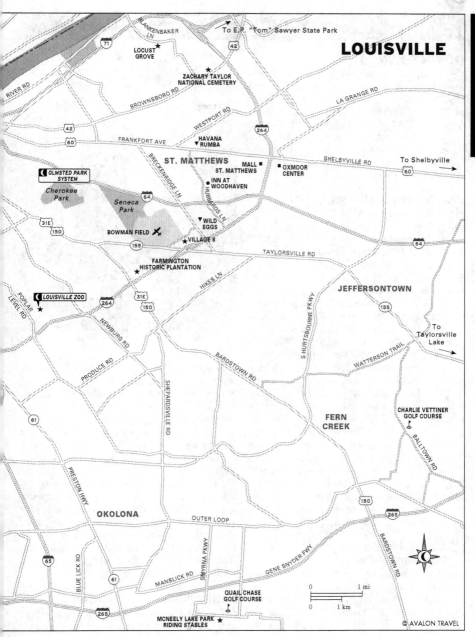

© AVALON TRAVEL

Sights

DOWNTOWN

Over the past two decades, Louisville's downtown has regained its title as the heart of the city. West Main Street's Museum Row (known as Whiskey Row in the early 1900s), stretching the four blocks from 5th to 9th Streets, can easily keep you busy for a weekend, if not a full week. Adding oomph to the experience is downtown's notable architecture, as well as the lively waterfront scene.

Frazier International History Museum

On the far western end of Museum Row, the Frazier International History Museum (829 W. Main St., 502/753-5663, www.fraziermuseum.org, 9 A.M.–5 P.M. Mon.–Sat., noon–5 P.M. Sun., $9.50 adults, $7.50 seniors, $6 youth 5–14) bears the honor of being the only place outside the United Kingdom to house a permanent exhibition of items from the Royal Armoury, the U.K.'s prized national collection of many centuries' worth of arms and armor. The museum's collections go far beyond the Armoury pieces, however, with Teddy Roosevelt's "Big Stick," Geronimo's bow, the Daniel Boone family bible, Lewis and Clark artifacts, and Frank and Jesse James's letters all finding homes at the Frazier. As impressive as the collections are, for many visitors they're overshadowed by the museum's 80 historical interpretations performed by a full-time staff of actor-historians. The over 1,000 years of history on display at the Frazier come to life as Annie Oakley, Abraham Lincoln, Joan of Arc, and other historical figures make appearances on the 1st floor stage or in the 3rd floor Tournament Ring.

◖ Louisville Slugger Museum & Factory

Louisville might not have a Major League Baseball team, but America's pastime wouldn't be the same if it weren't for the Louisville Slugger, the official baseball bat of MLB. On a tour of the Louisville Slugger Museum &

© THERESA DOWELL BLACKINTON

Louisville Slugger Museum & Factory

Factory (800 W. Main St., 877/775-8443, www.sluggermuseum.org, 9 A.M.–5 P.M. Mon.–Sat., noon–5 P.M. Sun., $10 adults, $9 seniors, $5 youth 6–12), visitors can learn how the history of baseball and the Louisville Slugger go step-in-step, take a practice swing with bats used by favorite players of the past and present, and tour the factory where each bat is made with as much love and care as in 1884, the year the Louisville Slugger was born. At the end of the tour, each participant receives a free miniature Louisville Slugger. Take it home with you (though only in your checked luggage!), after first posing with it in front of the world's largest bat, a 120-foot tall, 68,000-pound steel replica of a Babe Ruth bat that greets everyone walking past the museum.

Louisville Science Center

More than a field-trip destination where you can see a mummy and be enclosed in a bubble, the Louisville Science Center (727 W. Main St., 800/591-2203, www.louisville-science.org, 9:30 A.M.–5 P.M. Sun.–Thurs., 9:30 A.M.–9 P.M. Fri.–Sat., $12 adults, $10 youth 2–12) is an all-ages destination where science education meets hands-on fun. For the little ones under age seven, KidZone offers age-appropriate excitement, including occupation exploration via dress-up and a table of wet and wild construction fun. Older children will enjoy the over 150 learning stations in the museum's three permanent exhibitions—The

FAMOUS LOUISVILLIANS

Decking the sides of downtown buildings are large, hard-to-miss, black-and-white posters created by the Greater Louisville Pride Foundation to celebrate local legends. "Louisville's Ali" smiles down at drivers on River Road, while an image on East Main Street showing Pee Wee Reese with Jackie Robinson declares that this is "Pee Wee's Louisville." Look around and see how many of Louisville's celebrities you recognize. You might be surprised just who calls Louisville their hometown.

- Muhammad Ali: Three-time World Heavyweight Champion and Olympic gold medalist

- Louis Brandeis: Supreme Court Justice

- Lance Burton: Magician with his own Las Vegas show

- Jennifer Carpenter: Actress most famous for her role as Debra Morgan on *Dexter*

- Bob Edwards: Radio personality and first host of NPR's *Morning Edition*

- Dian Fossey: Primatologist famed for her study of mountain gorillas

- Sue Grafton: Author of the Kinsey Millhone mystery novels

- Darrell Griffith: NBA star with the Utah Jazz known as Dr. Dunkenstein

- Paul Hornung: Heisman trophy winner and Green Bay Packers star

- Allan Houston: NBA star with the Detroit Pistons and New York Knicks

- Tori Murden McClure: First woman to row solo across the Atlantic

- Mary T. Meagher Plant: Olympic gold medalist in swimming

- Pee Wee Reese: All-star baseball player for the Brooklyn and L.A. Dodgers

- Diane Sawyer: Television journalist and anchor of ABC's *World News*

- Phil Simms: Super Bowl-winning quarterback for the New York Giants

- Hunter S. Thompson: Father of gonzo journalism and novelist

© THERESA DOWELL BLACKINTON

Pee Wee Reese poster

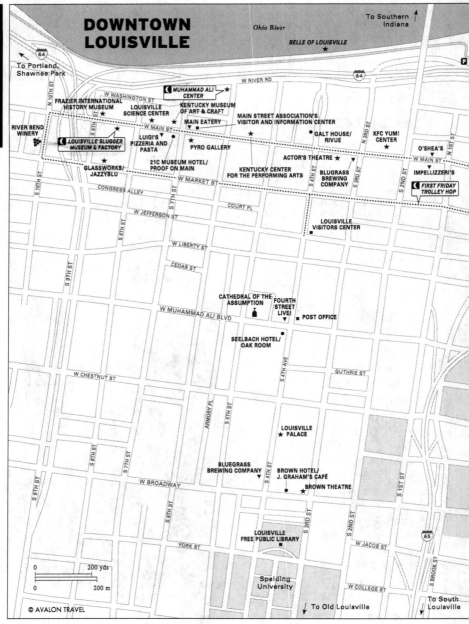

DOWNTOWN LOUISVILLE

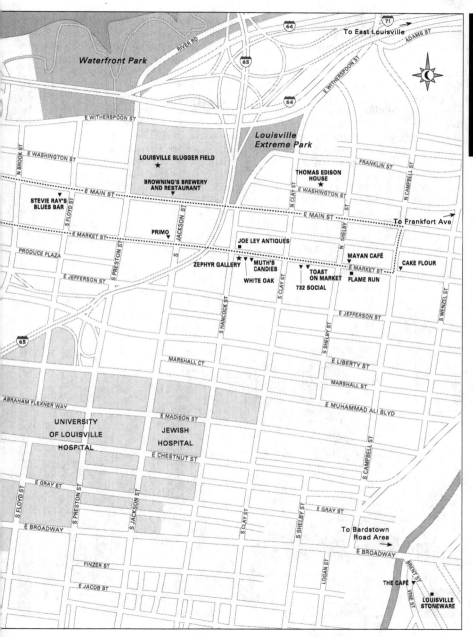

To East Louisville

Waterfront Park

River Rd

Louisville Extreme Park

E WITHERSPOON ST

E WASHINGTON ST

LOUISVILLE SLUGGER FIELD ★

THOMAS EDISON HOUSE ★

FRANKLIN ST

E MAIN ST

BROWNING'S BREWERY AND RESTAURANT ▼

E WASHINGTON ST

STEVIE RAY'S BLUES BAR ▼

E MAIN ST

To Frankfort Ave

E MARKET ST

PRIMO ▼

JOE LEY ANTIQUES ■

MAYAN CAFÉ ▼

CAKE FLOUR ▼

PRODUCE PLAZA

ZEPHYR GALLERY ★▼

MUTH'S CANDIES ▼

E MARKET ST

E JEFFERSON ST

WHITE OAK

TOAST ON MARKET ▼

FLAME RUN ■

732 SOCIAL

E JEFFERSON ST

MARSHALL CT

E LIBERTY ST

MARSHALL ST

ABRAHAM FLEXNER WAY

E MADISON ST

E MUHAMMAD ALI BLVD

UNIVERSITY OF LOUISVILLE HOSPITAL

JEWISH HOSPITAL

E CHESTNUT ST

E GRAY ST

E GRAY ST

E BROADWAY

To Bardstown Road Area

E BROADWAY

FINZER ST

THE CAFÉ

E JACOB ST

LOUISVILLE STONEWARE ■

World We Create, The World Within Us, and The World Around Us. The crawl-through cave and climb-aboard Gemini trainer space capsule are just a few of the favorites that encourage visitors to engage with the exhibits. Special exhibitions are rolled out every 3–4 months and often appeal to adults, as do many of the standing exhibits, such as the ones on healthy living. An IMAX theater ($5) with a four-story screen completes the museum. The $5 parking garage and on-site Subway restaurant make it easy to stay all day.

Kentucky Museum of Art & Craft

In a restored cast-iron building with cork floors and exposed beams, the Kentucky Museum of Art & Craft (715 W. Main St., 502/589-0102, www.kentuckyarts.org, 10 A.M.–5 P.M. Mon.–Fri., 11 A.M.–5 P.M. Sat., $6 adults and youth 12 and older, $5 seniors) celebrates the wealth of artistic talent and creativity found throughout the state. The museum's three galleries offer permanent and rotating exhibits featuring woodwork, textiles, ceramics, jewelry, photography, painting, and more. You'll likely find something you've never seen anywhere else and just have to have. Lucky for you some items on display are also for sale, and there's a gift shop next to the galleries.

21C Museum

Occupying the reception area and lower atrium of the hotel of the same name, the 21C Museum (700 W. Main St., 502/217-6300, www.21cmuseum.org, free) exhibits cutting-edge artwork from living artists. Exhibits change every six months, and the museum also offers a full program of film screenings, poetry readings, artist talks, and concert series. Pop in often—it's where the cool kids come to play—and don't forget to check out the elevator lobby as well as the restrooms. Art isn't restricted to the galleries here; it's an integral part of the entire building.

◖ Muhammad Ali Center

While most museums beg you to keep your hands off the exhibits, the Muhammad Ali Center (144 N. 6th St., 502/584-9254, www.alicenter.org, 9:30 A.M.–5 P.M. Tues.–Sat.,

Muhammad Ali Center

PUBLIC ART IN THE DERBY CITY

When you spot your first brightly painted horse sculpture, you might think it's nothing more than a nice touch from a local business, a way to brighten up the sidewalk and perhaps draw in a bit of business. When you start to see that these magnificent pieces of public art are all over town, you'll realize that there's something more to it. First appearing in the Derby City in 2004, the horses are part of a city fundraiser named **Gallopalooza** (www.gallopalooza.com). A second crop of horses, this time numbering 132, appeared in 2009. If you observe closely, you'll notice that the horses come in five different poses, from a relaxed horse in repose to a thoroughbred in mid-stride. Each horse is designed by a local artist and sponsored by a local business. The sponsors have the choice of purchasing their horse or putting it up for auction. Either way, all proceeds go to supporting Brightside, a local organization dedicated to beautifying the city. Stylistically, the horses range from the whimsical, such as Gogh, Starr, Gogh, a Van Gogh-style horse sponsored by ad agency Starr Promotions, to the serious, such as Flags-4-Vets-sponsored Black Jack, a tribute to the riderless horse that accompanied Presidents Kennedy, Hoover, and Johnson, as well as over 1,000 U.S. vets to their final resting place at Arlington National Cemetery. Images of all the horses, as well as a map showing where each is located, can be found at the Gallopalooza website.

depicting Ali's losses alongside his wins, his radical comments alongside his inspirational quotes, his contentious choices alongside his universally celebrated moments. On the three floors of exhibition space, you can view a five-screen orientation film, test your boxing skills with punching bags and in a shadowboxing ring, watch your choice of Ali's 15 most famous fights, and check out memorabilia from Ali's life and career.

KentuckyShow!

Want to get a taste of everything the great state of Kentucky has to offer before you dive into any deeper exploration? Then grab a seat at the KentuckyShow! (501 W. Main St., 502/562-7800, www.kentuckyshow.com, $7), a 30-minute multimedia production offered at the Kentucky Center for the Arts. Narrated by Kentuckian Ashley Judd, KentuckyShow! provides a moving look at Kentucky's history and culture, defining what makes the Bluegrass State such a special place. Screenings are offered on the house 11 A.M.–4 P.M. Tuesday–Saturday and 1–4 P.M. Sunday. Receive a $2 discount by showing your Louisville Free Public Library membership card.

Thomas Edison House

Before he invented the lightbulb, Thomas Edison was a Western Union telegraph operator in Louisville. The small four-room boarding house where he lived during that period, 1866–1867, is now the Thomas Edison House (729 E. Washington St., 502/585-5247, www.historichomes.org/edisonhouse, 10 A.M.–2 P.M. Tues.–Sat., $5 adults, $4 seniors, $3 youth 5–18). On a short tour of the property, visitors see his re-created room and can take a close look at a number of his inventions, including a working telegraph and working phonograph.

Riverboat Cruises

The oldest river steamboat in operation, the *Belle of Louisville* (401 W. River Rd., 502/574-2992, www.belleoflouisville.org, May–Oct.) is both a National Landmark and a local icon. Using her big red paddlewheel, the *Belle* carries

noon–5 P.M. Sun., $9 adults, $8 seniors, $5 students, $4 youth 6–12) repeatedly asks you to "Please Touch." This hands-on, full sensory, multimedia-heavy museum is a look at the life and times of The Greatest, a tribute to a hometown hero who became a universal icon. Far from one-sided, the Center depicts Ali the boxer, Ali the poet, and Ali the humanitarian, and it does not shy away from controversy,

the Louisville Free Public Library's main branch

© THERESA DOWELL BLACKINTON

passengers up and down the Ohio River, offering exceptional city views all to the tune of her distinctive calliope. Choose between excursion, lunch, dinner, or dance cruises; then step onboard and be transported back to the age of riverboat transport.

The Belle's sister boat, the *Spirit of Jefferson*, is a newer and smaller riverboat with modern conveniences that allow it to operate year-round. See the Belle of Louisville website for schedules for both boats, as well as information on special event cruises. Price depends on the type of cruise chosen.

Notable Architecture

Louisville's West Main Street is second only to NYC's SoHo in the number of cast-iron facade buildings. The eight-block area is also home to Greek Revival, Italianate, Richardsonian Romanesque, international, and postmodern architecture. Pick up a Walking Tour brochure from the Main Street Association's Visitor and Information Center (627 W. Main St., 502/568-2220, www.mainstreetassociation. com, 11 A.M.–3 P.M. Mon.–Fri.) and explore

the history and style that makes this one of Louisville's most architecturally interesting areas. Highlights include Mies van der Rohe's "rusted" American Life and Accident Building (3 Riverfront Plaza), Michael Graves's postmodern Humana Building (500 W. Main St.), and the abundance of cast-iron buildings in the 600 and 700 blocks of West Main.

The gothic revival **Cathedral of the Assumption** (433 S. 5th St., 502/582-2971, www.cathedraloftheassumption.org) is the home of the Archdiocese of Louisville and a downtown landmark. Built in 1852, the cathedral was completely renovated in 1994. It boasts one of the oldest American-made stained-glass windows as well as a beautiful starred ceiling complete with restored fresco.

The collections at the **main branch of the Louisville Free Public Library** (301 York St., 502/574-1611, www.lfpl.org, 9 A.M.–9 P.M. Mon.–Thurs., 9 A.M.–5 P.M. Fri.–Sat.) are not limited to books and magazines, but also include photos and artifacts related to local history. Even if you're not a bibliophile, the library is worth a visit for a look at the South

JUST ACROSS THE BRIDGE: SIGHTS IN SOUTHERN INDIANA

Cross the Ohio River, and you'll find yourself in southern Indiana, which is for all intents and purposes a suburb of Louisville. A handful of interesting sights make a trip across the state line worthwhile.

Falls of the Ohio State Park & Interpretive Center (201 Riverside Dr., Clarksville, IN, 812/280-9970, www.fallsoftheohio.org, 9 A.M.-5 P.M. Mon.-Sat., 1-5 P.M. Sun., $5 adults, $2 youth) welcomes visitors to wander among 386-million-year-old fossil beds and search the 220 acres for signs of life from the Devonian period. The Interpretive Center hosts 100 different exhibits focusing on paleontology, geology, and history. A 14-minute movie, aquarium with fish found in the Ohio River, and a full-size mammoth skeleton are visitor favorites. If you just want to wander among the fossils or have a picnic at river's edge, the park itself is open 7 A.M.-11 P.M., and you must pay only a $2 parking fee.

Enjoy a night out at **Derby Dinner Playhouse** (525 Marriott Dr., Clarksville, IN, 812/288-8281, www.derbydinner.com), a dinner theater that specializes in productions of Broadway musicals, having put on all 50 of the top musicals of all time. There are no bad seats at the in-the-square theater, and a vocal ensemble entertains you as you enjoy your buffet dinner. Performances are held Tuesday–Sunday evenings with matinees on Wednesday and Sunday. Ticket prices range from $33 to $42.

The **Howard Steamboat Museum** (1101 E. Market St., Jeffersonville, IN, 812/283-3728, www.steamboatmuseum.org, 10 A.M.-4 P.M. Tues.-Sat., 1-4 P.M. Sun., $5 adults, $4 seniors, $3 students) invites you to return to the golden era of steamboat travel on a tour through the 1894 mansion of the steamboat magnate Howard family. Models of steamboats, photographs, and artifacts are found throughout the grand house.

The **Carnegie Center for Art & History** (201 E. Spring St., New Albany, IN, 812/944-7336, www.carnegiecenter.org, 10 A.M.-5:30 P.M. Tues.-Sat., free) features an award-winning exhibit on the Underground Railroad as well as a smile-inducing collection of hand-carved, mechanized dioramas depicting rural life at the end of the 19th century. Each year the center also hosts a juried art quilt exhibition, drawing entries from contemporary fiber artists across the country.

A visit to **Huber's Orchard, Winery, & Vineyards** (19816 Huber Rd., Starlight, IN, 812/923-9463, www.huberwinery.com, 10 A.M.-6 P.M. Mon.-Sat., noon-6 P.M. Sun.) is an annual tradition for many locals, especially during apple- and pumpkin-picking seasons. Year-round you can take a complimentary wine tour with tasting (11 A.M. and 2 P.M. daily), purchase produce at the farm market, and enjoy a hearty farm meal at the Starlight Café. From May through October, a Farm Park with rope mazes and mini tractor rides welcomes kids.

Building. Built in 1906 with funds from Andrew Carnegie, the beaux arts building features Ionic columns, ornamental friezes, marble floors, bronze doors, and large-scale mosaics and paintings.

Portland

Located a bit west of downtown at the Falls of the Ohio, the current neighborhood of Portland was once an independent town and an important stop for riverboat traffic. Though the area has seen some hard times in the past decades, many Louisville old-timers have fond memories of Portland, and notable Louisvillians such as football great Paul Hornung grew up in the neighborhood. **The Portland Museum** (2308 Portland Ave., 502/776-7678, www.go-portland.org, 10 A.M.–4:30 P.M. Tues.–Thurs., $7 adults, $6 seniors, $5 students) explores the history of the land, river, and people who called Portland home and helped turn Louisville from a shipping port into a city.

A light-and-sound-enhanced exhibit with detailed dioramas and lifelike human models tells the story of Portland, while additional galleries host rotating exhibits that illuminate life in this vibrant and historic district.

OLD LOUISVILLE

Home to the largest collection of Victorian mansions in the United States and showcasing a variety of impressive architectural styles of the late 19th and early 20th centuries, Old Louisville is a spirited neighborhood rich in history and perfect for on-foot exploration. It's also where you'll find the University of Louisville, which helps keep this old neighborhood young, hip, and richly diverse.

◖ Old Louisville Tours

To get the most out of a visit to Old Louisville, consider a tour. Do-it-yourselfers can choose from five self-guided walking/driving tours outlined in brochures produced by the **Old Louisville Visitors Center** (218 W. Oak St., 502/637-2922, www.oldlouisville.org, 9 A.M.–5 P.M. Tues.–Sat.). Those looking for a real insider's view should sign up for one of the outings with Louisville Historic Tours (502/637-2922, www.louisvillehistorictours.com), which employs neighborhood residents as guides. Guided walking tours include the Old Louisville Grand Walking Tour (11 A.M. and 3 P.M. Tues.–Sat., $15), the Old Louisville Ghost Walk (1 P.M. Tues.–Thurs. and Sat., $20), and the Lantern Ghost Walk (7 P.M. daily, $25). Guided bus tours include the Mansions & Milestones Tour (2:30 P.M. Fri.–Sat., $25), and the Ghosts of Old Louisville Tour (7:30 P.M. Fri., $25). Tours depart from the Old Louisville Visitors Center and last 1.5–2 hours. Reservations are recommended. For a chance to peek inside some of the neighborhood beauties, put the Holiday House Tour (www.holidayhousetour.com, $25), held annually on the first weekend of December, on your calendar. The Hidden Treasure Garden Tour (www.oldlouisvillegardentour.com, $15), held annually in early July, offers a look at what's behind the wrought-iron fences of many neighborhood homes.

Conrad-Caldwell House

Of the many historic homes in Louisville, the Conrad-Caldwell House (1402 St. James Ct., 502/636-5023, www.conradcaldwell.org, noon–4 P.M. Wed.–Fri. and Sun., 10 A.M.–4 P.M. Sat., $5 adults, $4 seniors, $3 students), a grand three-story Victorian mansion from the 1890s, might just be the most interesting to tour. Named for Theophilus Conrad, who built and occupied the house for its first 10 years, and the William E. Caldwell family, who lived in the house through the 1920s, the house boasts beautiful parquet floors patterned after quilts; a remarkable attention to detail in the woodworked walls, staircases, and decorative features; and original furniture, books, and belongings from the Caldwell family. If you're lucky, you'll be guided through the house by a direct descendant of William Caldwell, bursting with intimate knowledge of the family and great stories about the house.

© THERESA DOWELL BLACKINTON

Conrad-Caldwell House

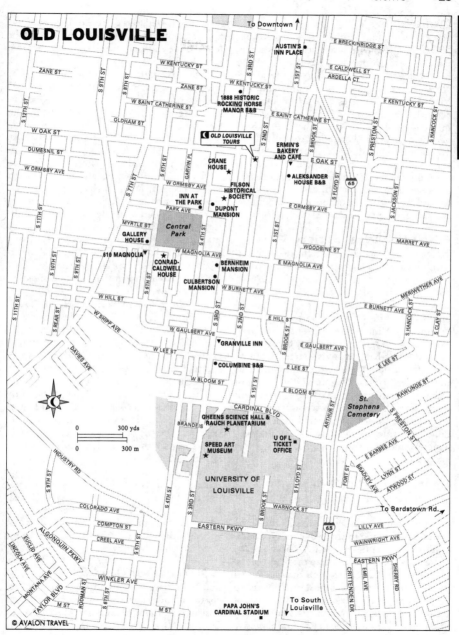

OLD LOUISVILLE

To Downtown

E BRECKINRIDGE ST

AUSTIN'S
INN PLACE

E CALDWELL ST
ARDELLA CT

ZANE ST

W KENTUCKY ST

ZANE ST

W KENTUCKY ST

E KENTUCKY ST

W SAINT CATHERINE ST

1888 HISTORIC
ROCKING HORSE
MANOR B&B

OLDHAM ST

E SAINT CATHERINE ST

W OAK ST

OLD LOUISVILLE
TOURS

DUMESNIL ST

ERMIN'S
BAKERY
AND CAFÉ

E OAK ST

W ORMSBY AVE

CRANE
HOUSE

ALEKSANDER
HOUSE B&B

65

FILSON
HISTORICAL
SOCIETY

INN AT
THE PARK

DUPONT
MANSION

E ORMSBY AVE

PARK AVE

MYRTLE ST

GALLERY
HOUSE

Central
Park

WOODBINE ST

MARRET AVE

618 MAGNOLIA

W MAGNOLIA AVE

E MAGNOLIA AVE

CONRAD-
CALDWELL
HOUSE

BERNHEIM
MANSION

CULBERTSON
MANSION

MERIWETHER AVE

W BURNETT AVE

W HILL ST

E HILL ST

E BURNETT AVE

W SHIPP AVE

W GAULBERT AVE

GRANVILLE INN

E GAULBERT AVE

W LEE ST

E LEE ST

St.
Stephens
Cemetery

DAVIES AVE

COLUMBINE B&B

W BLOOM ST

E BLOOM ST

CARDINAL BLVD

GHEENS SCIENCE HALL &
RAUCH PLANETARIUM

BRANDEIS

0   300 yds

0   300 m

SPEED ART
MUSEUM

U OF L
TICKET
OFFICE

E BARBEE AVE

INDUSTRY RD

UNIVERSITY OF
LOUISVILLE

To Bardstown Rd.

COLORADO AVE

LILLY AVE

COMPTON ST

EASTERN PKWY

WAINWRIGHT AVE

CREEL AVE

EASTERN PKWY

65

ALGONQUIN PKWY

EUCLID AVE

LINCOLN AVE

WINKLER AVE

MONTANA AVE

TAYLOR BLVD

M ST

M ST

PAPA JOHN'S
CARDINAL STADIUM

To South
Louisville

© AVALON TRAVEL

Crane House

Since 1987, Crane House (1244 S. 3rd St., 502/635-2240, www.cranehouse.org, 9 A.M.–5 P.M., Mon.–Fri.) has been exposing Louisville residents and visitors to the culture of East Asia through a variety of programming. Visitors are welcome to take a free tour (reservations requested) of Crane House, which includes a visit to the Asia Gallery, an exhibit of contemporary and historical Asian artifacts, as well as an introduction to Chinese tea and tea drinking. Crane House also offers Chinese cooking classes, Chinese and Japanese language classes, and Tai Chi classes. A regular lecture series is free and open to the public; check the online calendar.

Filson Historical Society

Home to extensive library collections chronicling local and Southern history, the Filson Historical Society (1310 S. 3rd St., 502/635-5083, www.filsonhistorical.org, 9 A.M.–5 P.M. Mon.–Fri., free) is a gem for researchers. The excellent lecture series is also a boon to the community. Visit the website for a schedule of events. The Ferguson Mansion, home of the Society, is worth a visit on its own merit. A self-guided tour describes the luxurious elements that made this beaux-arts mansion the most expensive house in the city when it was built in 1905 and also allows visitors to view many of the Society's artifacts, including a carving done by Daniel Boone, Civil War uniforms, a moonshine still, antique quilts, and a strong art collection.

University of Louisville

The University of Louisville, a public university, bustles with the energy of over 22,000 students, who come from around the state, country, and world to study in over 170 fields. The urban campus is not just for students, however; it also offers much to the community. Go ahead and take a stroll on the manicured grounds of Belknap Campus. You'll want to keep an eye out for one of the original casts of Rodin's *The Thinker,* which sits eternally lost in thought in front of the main administrative

building, as well as the grave of U.S. Supreme Court Justice Louis Brandeis, which can be found under the portico of the law school that bears his name.

One of the most visited on-campus sites by the public is the **Speed Art Museum** (2035 S. 3rd St., 502/634-2700, www.speedmuseum.org, 10 A.M.–5 P.M. Wed–Thurs. and Sat., 10 A.M.–9 P.M. Fri., noon–5 P.M. Sun., free), home to Louisville's best art collection, with over 13,000 works spanning 6,000 years. Along with impressionist paintings by Monet, modernist creations by Matisse, and pop art masterpieces by Warhol, you'll also find collections featuring African, Native American, and Kentucky artwork. Be sure to stop in the English Renaissance Room, where the panels from a 1619 British country house featuring scenes from Ovid's *Metamorphoses* rival the art on display. Children will love ArtSparks ($5), a hands-on environment where they can let out their inner artist.

The nearby **Gheens Science Hall & Rauch Planetarium** (108 W. Brandeis Ave., 502/852-6664; www.louisville.edu/planetarium, $7 adults, $5 seniors and youth 12 and under) exposes the public to the wonders of space through a wide range of shows illuminating the night sky, the planets, our solar system, and far beyond. Locals might particularly enjoy the seasonal Skies over Louisville program, which explains exactly what it is you're seeing in the sky right over your own backyard. For something a bit less expected, check out the laser shows, which are set to the tunes of the Beatles, Led Zeppelin, Radiohead, and other popular bands. Shows are generally offered at 8 P.M., 9 P.M., 10 P.M., and 11 P.M. Friday and at 11 A.M., noon, and 1 P.M. on Saturday, though additional shows are often added to the schedule. Check the website for complete show listings.

SOUTH LOUISVILLE

South Louisville has had a bit of a roller-coaster existence, soaring in the late 19th and first half of the 20th centuries as Churchill Downs and Iroquois Park laid claim to the area and a railcar line made the connection to downtown simple, then falling in the late 1900s as the factories that employed many of the area's middle-class workers left town. Now, this area, once a summer retreat and still the location of some of the city's most historic sites and homes, is again on the way up. A favorite area for new immigrants, South Louisville mixes local tradition with newly introduced customs.

Kentucky Kingdom

Whether you prefer the shake, rattle, and roll of wooden roller coasters or the relaxation of a Ferris wheel, Kentucky Kingdom (Crittenden Dr., Kentucky Exposition Center, 800/727-3267, Apr.–Oct.) appeals to the amusement park aficionado in all of us. Part of the Six Flag chains from 1998 to 2009, the park closed for the 2010 season as it transitioned back to its original local management. The new owners intend to reopen Kentucky Kingdom in 2012 with an expanded waterpark and most of the same rides and attractions. Season passes offer the best value.

◖ Kentucky Derby Museum and Churchill Downs

If you can't make it to the Derby, experiencing the thrill of the most exciting two minutes in sports on the 360-degree high-definition screen at the Kentucky Derby Museum (704 Central Ave., 502/637-7097, www.derbymuseum. org, 8 A.M.–5 P.M. Mon.–Sat., 11 A.M.–5 P.M. Sun. Mar. 15–Nov., 9 A.M.–5 P.M. Mon.–Sat., 11 A.M.–5 P.M. Sun. Dec.–Mar. 14, $13 adults, $12 seniors, $11 youth 13–18, $5 youth 5–12) is the next best thing. In addition to the film, interactive exhibits and authentic artifacts allow you to get a taste of Derby Day, discover what it takes to create a champion thoroughbred, and learn about the pursuit of victory from the perspective of jockey, trainer, and owner. The museum was damaged extensively by flooding in early 2009, and while closed for recovery, museum exhibits were overhauled and updated. Your admission ticket also allows you to take a guided walking tour of Churchill Downs, the racetrack where the Derby is run every May under the famed twin spires. For a more in-depth look at the historic track, the museum

© THERESA DOWELL BLACKINTON

approaching the finish line at Churchill Downs

also offers a Behind the Scenes Walking Tour ($10), a Barn & Backside Van Tour ($10), and a Horses & Haunts Tour ($15).

Little Loomhouse

Preserving the legacy of Lou Tate, a master weaver whose work was admired by the likes of first ladies Eleanor Roosevelt and Lou Hoover, the Little Loomhouse (328 Kenwood Hill Rd., 502/367-4792, www.littleloomhouse. org, 10 A.M.–3:30 P.M. Tues.–Thurs. and 3rd Sat. of the month, $3.50) offers tours of her home and workshop. You'll step foot in the cabin where "Happy Birthday" was first sung,

---

THE BIRTH OF THE HAPPY BIRTHDAY SONG

There are some things that seem as if they've simply always been, the Happy Birthday song a fine example of that. Sung to us annually by friends and family to mark the passing of another year, and memorably spiced up by Marilyn Monroe for President Kennedy, "Happy Birthday to You" is so omnipresent in our society, that health care officials even suggest we sing it as we wash our hands to ensure that we scrub for the proper amount of time needed to kill germs.

But once upon a time, not long before the 19th century turned to the 20th, the Happy Birthday song did not exist. How they celebrated birthdays then, heaven knows, but apparently they did still have parties, because it was at a birthday celebration on what is now the Little Loomhouse property in South Louisville that sisters Patty and Mildred J. Hill introduced the song for the first time. Both kindergarten teachers, the sisters had originally written in 1893 a song called "Good Morning to All," which was well loved by their students. By keeping the melody and simply changing the simple lyrics, the Hill sisters created history and made birthdays better for all of us.

---

see samples of the intricate patterns Lou Tate helped preserve, and learn to weave on a little loom. More in-depth weaving classes are also offered in multi-week sessions. An active participant in South Louisville life, the Little Loomhouse gift shop sells a guidebook to the surrounding neighborhood that will allow you to better explore the area.

Waverly Hills Sanatorium

If your idea of a good time is having the living daylights scared out of you, then add Waverly Hills Sanatorium (4400 Paralee Ln., 502/933-2142, www.therealwaverlyhills.com) to your must-see list. This former tuberculosis healthcare facility and geriatric center is said to be one of the most haunted sites in the United States. For those brave enough, the sanatorium offers half-night (midnight–4 A.M. Fri., Mar.–Aug., $50) and full-night (midnight–8 A.M. Sat., Mar.–Aug., $100) paranormal investigations that are said to have turned up sightings of ghosts, ectoplasm clouds, and lights where there is no electricity, as well as the sounds of voices, cries, screams, slamming doors, and bouncing balls. If just reading this makes you want to hide under a blanket, then opt for the two-hour historical tour (2:30 P.M. Sun. Mar.–Aug., 8 P.M. Wed. Sept.–Oct., $22). All tours must be reserved in advance and are often booked months in advance. Proceeds fund the restoration of the building.

Riverside, The Farnsley-Moremen Landing

Experience life at a 19th-century Ohio River farm on a visit to Riverside, The Farnsley-Moremen Landing (7410 Moorman Rd., 502/935-6809, www.riverside-landing.org, 10 A.M.–4:30 P.M. Tues.–Sat., 1–4:30 P.M. Sun., final tour at 3:30, $6 adults, $5 seniors, $3 youth 5–12), a popular stop for boat traffic back when the river was equivalent to today's interstate. A tour will take you into the house, remarkable for its two-story Greek Revival portico. You'll notice that it's decorated in two different styles: the first floor re-creates life in 1840 when Gabriel Farnsley lived in the house as a bachelor, the second draws its style from 1880 when three generations of the Moremen family occupied the house. You'll also visit the detached kitchen, as well as the kitchen garden, where volunteers grow plants that very likely would have been served at mealtime in the 1800s. Be sure to enjoy the view of the river from the grounds; it's photo worthy.

FRANKFORT AVENUE AND EAST LOUISVILLE

Frankfort Avenue, running east from downtown, is a lively neighborhood more known for its restaurants and shopping than its attractions, though it's easy to spend a day exploring the area and enjoying the ambiance. Once the gateway between Frankfort (hence the name) and Louisville, Frankfort Avenue is chock a block with historic buildings that have maintained their style despite finding new uses. Continuing east from Frankfort Avenue, you'll find yourself in East Louisville, a popular residential area that also houses interesting sights, primarily historical. With amorphous boundaries—you'll get a lot of different answers if you ask a local just what East Louisville includes—the sights in this section are located as close as five minutes and as distant as thirty minutes from downtown.

American Printing House for the Blind

The museum of the American Printing House for the Blind (1839 Frankfort Ave., 502/895-2405, www.aph.org, 8:30 A.M.–4:30 P.M. Mon.–Fri., 10 A.M.–3 P.M. Sat., free), the oldest and largest producer of materials for the visually impaired, contains hands-on exhibits that document the evolution of tactile reading systems for the blind and contains items such as a 142-volume Braille translation of an encyclopedia, a Braille bible used by Helen Keller, and a variety of Braille typewriters you can try out. For a more in-depth look at the fascinating work done by the APH, take a free tour (10 A.M. and 2 P.M. Mon.–Thurs.), where you'll get to see the printing press in action and listen in on the recording of Talking Books.

Whitehall

Though it began its life as a modest red-brick Italianate farmhouse, Whitehall (3110 Lexington Rd., 502/897-2944, www.historichomes.org/whitehall, 10 A.M.–2 P.M. Mon.–Fri., $5 adults, $4 seniors, $3 youth 6–18) grew from its humble 1855 origins to become an imposing Southern-style Greek Revival mansion. On a tour of its 15 rooms, you'll learn the history of the home and see the elaborate stylings introduced by the home's two most prominent owners. The Middleton family, who bought the house in 1909, renovated it into the style we see today, while the Hume family, who occupied the house from 1924 to 1992, made the necessary arrangements for Whitehall to become a historic property. Intricate fireplaces and wood floors, period wallpaper, and beautifully carved furniture imported from around the world give Whitehall its sumptuous feel. Don't forget to check out the formal gardens, a popular spot for weddings.

Louisville Visual Art Association

Acting as an advocate since the dawn of the 20th century for the importance of arts in building community and culture, the Louisville Visual Art Association (3005 River Rd., 502/896-2146, www.louisvillevisualart.org, 9 A.M.–5 P.M. Mon.–Fri., noon–4 P.M. Sun., free) locates itself in the Water Tower, a white columned, 19th-century structure on the bank of the Ohio River. Inside the impressive Greek Revival building, you'll find two galleries, each of which hosts rotating art exhibits. The galleries encourage visits with exhibition guides as well as children's activity sheets, each designed to make the current exhibit more accessible, no matter your level of familiarity with art.

Zachary Taylor National Cemetery

Originally the family burial grounds of the 12th President of the United States, Zachary Taylor National Cemetery (4701 Brownsboro Rd., 502/893-3852, www.cem.va.gov,

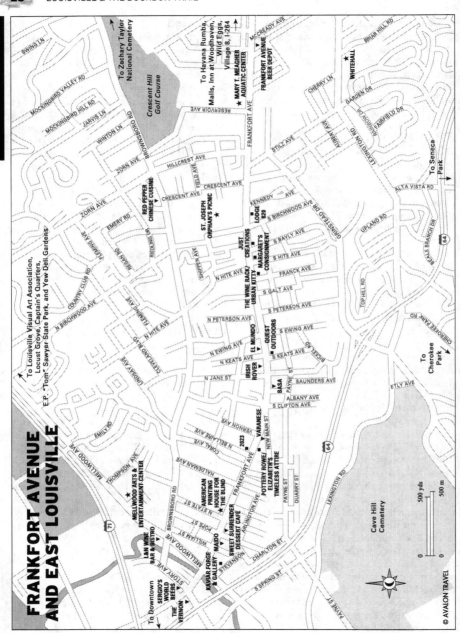

FRANKFORT AVENUE AND EAST LOUISVILLE

© AVALON TRAVEL

sunrise–sunset daily) was given federal status in 1928, 78 years after Old Rough and Ready was laid to rest. Now joining President Taylor and his family in eternal rest are U.S. military members who served the nation in the years ranging from the Spanish-American War to the Persian Gulf War. A life-size statue atop a 50-foot granite monument marks the grave of the Kentuckian cum president.

Locust Grove

Visited by three presidents as well as the returning Lewis and Clark, and lived in by Louisville founder George Rogers Clark for the last nine years of his life, Locust Grove (561 Blankenbaker Ln., 502/897-9845, www. locustgrove.org, 10 A.M.–4:30 P.M. Mon.–Sat., 1–4:30 P.M. Sun., last tour at 3:15 P.M., $8 adults, $7 seniors, $4 youth 12 and under) has played host to more than its share of history. Now this carefully restored 18th-century Georgian mansion, its grounds, formal gardens, and out buildings, are open to the public. A visit begins with a short film at quarter past the hour and then moves on to a 45-minute tour of the property, followed by a chance to explore the museum. You'll learn about early Kentucky history, westward expansion, frontier life, and slave life all while enjoying the beautiful setting. Each December, special holiday candlelight tours are offered, giving visitors a taste of an old-fashioned Christmas.

Yew Dell Gardens

Recognized by the Garden Conservancy for its exceptional nature, Yew Dell Gardens (6220 Old Lagrange Rd., Crestwood, 502/241-4788, www.yewdellgardens.org, 10 A.M.–4 P.M. Mon.–Sat., noon–4 P.M. Sun., Apr.–Nov., 10 A.M.–4 P.M. Mon.–Fri., Dec.–Mar., $7 adults and youth 12 and older, $5 seniors) is 33 acres of bliss for anyone who loves plants and remarkable landscaping. The once private gardens of renowned horticulturist Theodore Klein, who died in 1998, opened to the public in 2005. Visitors can now marvel at the more than 1,000 specimens of rare trees and shrubs in his arboretum as well as explore a variety of themed gardens. Favorites include the Secret Garden, the formal Topiary Garden, the English Walled Garden, the summertime Bloom Garden, and the evergreen Serpentine Garden.

BARDSTOWN ROAD AREA

For many residents of Louisville, Bardstown Road, which runs south from downtown toward the suburbs, perfectly sums up the Derby City. As with Frankfort Avenue, Bardstown Road is a happening hub, that despite not having too many tourist attractions per se, is a place where you could easily pass an entire day. It's the place to experience a Louisvillian's Louisville.

Cave Hill Cemetery

Cave Hill Cemetery (701 Baxter Ave., 502/451-5630, www.cavehillcemetery.com, 8 A.M.–4:45 P.M. daily) is not just a burial ground; it's also an arboretum, a masterpiece of landscape architecture, and a sculpture park. While strolling the grounds, you can admire the artwork

Colonel Sanders's grave at Cave Hill Cemetery

© THERESA DOWELL BLACKINTON

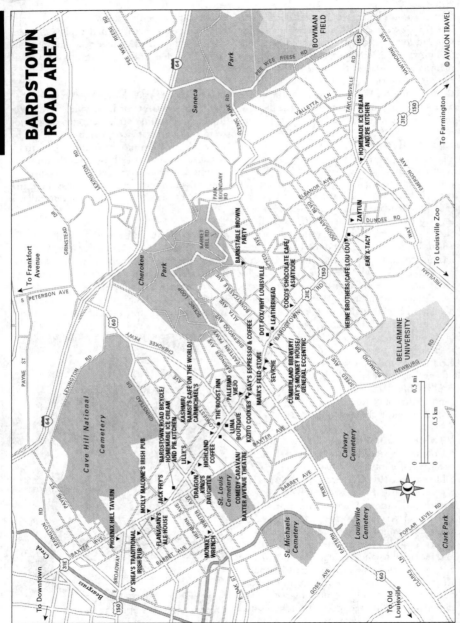

BARDSTOWN
ROAD AREA

© AVALON TRAVEL

adorning graves, identify over 500 species of tree and shrub, and feed the waterfowl that live on the lake. Don't forget to pay your respects to Colonel Sanders (section 33, marked with a bust) and other Kentucky notables such as city founder George Rogers Clark (section P). In the spring and fall, historical and geological tours are offered; visit the website for dates and fees.

Farmington Historic Plantation

Farmington (3033 Bardstown Rd., 502/452-9920, www.historichomes.org/farmington, 10 A.M.–4 P.M. Tues.–Sat., $9 adults, $8 seniors, $4 youth 5–18), the Federal-style home that sits at the heart of a former hemp plantation owned by the venerable Speed family, gives visitors a peek into genteel life in the early 1800s. Known for their philanthropic giving around Louisville, the Speed family had ties to both Thomas Jefferson and Abraham Lincoln, and Farmington gives special attention to the family's relationship with the latter. A permanent exhibition explores what life was like at Farmington when Lincoln spent three weeks there in 1841, and details his relationships with Joshua Speed, who he called his "most intimate friend," and James Speed, who served as Lincoln's attorney general. Another permanent exhibition details the lives of slaves at Farmington. Try to time your visit to coincide one of their reenactments, which really bring history to life.

◖ Louisville Zoo

With its nationally recognized four-acre Gorilla Forest as well as its groundbreaking Islands exhibit that allows Sumatran tigers, orangutans, tapirs, siamangs, and babirusas to rotate through different enclosures, the Louisville Zoo (1100 Trevilian Way, 502/459-2181, www.

louisvillezoo.org, 10 A.M.–4 P.M. daily Sep.–Feb., 10 A.M.–5 P.M. daily Mar.–Aug., extended summer hours, $12.95 adults, $9.50 seniors & youth 3–11) is one of the best zoos in the country. Follow the simple loop layout to catch all 1,300 residents of the zoo, ranging from the tiny frogs of the Amazonian rainforest to the giant elephants of the African plains. Regularly scheduled training and feeding programs add to the experience, as do the natural settings and informational panels. Glacier Run, a state-of-the-art home for the polar bears and their arctic companions, is new as of 2011. If you're around in October, throw on a costume and join the World's Largest Halloween Party, a favorite annual event.

© THERESA DOWELL BLACKINTON

leopard at the Louisville Zoo

Entertainment and Events

BARS AND CLUBS

Louisville has a happening bar and club scene that centers around three areas: downtown, Frankfort Avenue, and the Bardstown Road/Baxter Avenue corridor. Downtown draws more out-of-towners, while Frankfort Avenue and Bardstown Road host more locals, but you won't feel out of place in either locale. Vibes range from neighborhood joint to swanky club, but there's not an exclusive spot in town. While most cities go dark around 2 A.M., Louisville is unique in that most bars don't shut down until 4 A.M. on weekends.

Downtown

Louisville's downtown destination, **Fourth Street Live!** (400 S. 4th St., www.4thstlive.com), offers nightlife for every taste. For a more low-key and upscale night, sit back in a leather chair and sip one of the 60 bourbons on offer at **Maker's Mark Bourbon House & Lounge** (502/568-9009, www.makerslounge.com, 11 A.M.–midnight Mon.–Thurs., 11 A.M.–3 A.M. Fri.–Sat., 5 P.M.–midnight Sun.). If you're looking to party, choose between **Angel's Rock Bar** (502/540-1461, www.angelsrockbar-ky.com, 10 P.M.–4 A.M. Thurs.–Sat.), where hot DJs and live music keep the dance floor packed all night long, **Hotel Nightclub** (502/540-1116, www.hotel-ky.com, 10 P.M.–4 A.M. Thurs.–Sat.), the glam place to see and be seen, and **Saddle Ridge** (502/569-3507, www.saddleridgelouisville.com, 5 P.M.–4 A.M. Wed.–Sat.), where a mix of country, rock, and Top 40 encourages a diverse crowd to get wild saloon-style. These, and the other restaurants and bars that make up Fourth Street Live!, are all in one complex, so it's easy to check out the scene at each before deciding where to spend your night.

With the Fall 2010 opening of Louisville's new downtown arena, KFC Yum! Center, the area near Main and 2nd Streets is seeing rapid growth. **O' Shea's** (123 W. Main St., 502/708-2488, www.osheaslouisville.net, 11 A.M.–midnight Sun.–Thurs., 11 A.M.–4 A.M. Fri.–Sat.), a long-time favorite Louisville bar with an original location on Bardstown Road, the **Bluegrass Brewing Company** (3rd & Main Sts., 502/599-7981, www.bbcbrew.com, 11 A.M.–11 P.M. Mon.–Thurs., 11 A.M.–1 A.M. Fri.–Sat.), known for its microbrews, and **Impellizzeri's** (110 W. Main St., www.impellizzeris.com, 4–11 P.M. Mon.–Thurs., 11 A.M.–midnight Fri.–Sat.), a popular pizza place, were the first to stake their claim to the area, and more establishments are expected to follow.

For a less ordinary night out, center your plans around **River Bend Winery** (120 S. 10th St., 502/540-5650, www.riverbendwine.com, 10 A.M.–10 P.M. Mon.–Thurs., 10 A.M.–midnight Fri.–Sat., 1–6 P.M. Sun.). Though the fact that they produce a fine selection of wines made exclusively from Kentucky grapes is enough to make River Bend cool, the winery goes beyond offering the typical tours

© MATTHEW DOWELL

Fourth Street Live!

THE URBAN BOURBON TRAIL

For many people traveling Kentucky's Bourbon Trail, Louisville is the jumping-off point. If you arrive in town early and want to get a head start on the sampling, check out Louisville's Urban Bourbon Trail, a collection of nine bars that have quality selections of bourbon.

- The Bar at Blu (280 W. Jefferson St., 502/627-5045, www.blugrille.com)

- Baxter Station (1201 Payne St., 502/584-1635, www.baxterstation.com)

- Bourbons Bistro (2255 Frankfort Ave., 502/894-8838, www.bourbonsbistro. com)

- The Brown Hotel Bar (335 W. Broadway, 502/324-1289, www.brownhotel.com)

- Jockey Silks Bourbon Bar (140 N. 4th St., 502/589-5200, www.galthouse.com)

- Maker's Mark Bourbon House & Lounge (446 S. 4th St., 502/568-9009, www.makerslounge.com)

- The Old Seelbach Bar (500 S. 4th St., 502/585-3200, www.seelbachhilton.com)

- Proof on Main (700 W. Main St., 502/217-6360, www.proofonmain.com)

- Z's Fusion (115 S. 4th St., 502/855-8000, www.zsfusion.com)

and tastings (which are available every day) to hosting fun events. It's a happening place every night of the week with Latin dancing on Monday (lessons at 8 P.M., open floor at 9 P.M.); swing dancing (lessons at 7 P.M., open floor at 8 P.M.), open mic comedy (8:30 P.M.), and $10 all-you-can-drink wine on Tuesday; $2 glasses of wine on Wednesday; wine and yoga on Thursday (6 P.M.); and live music all weekend. If the joint is jumping, they'll stay open past stated closing hours.

Frankfort Avenue

The Vernon (1575 Story Ave., 502/584-8460, www.vernonclub.com, 5 P.M.–midnight Tues. and Thurs., 5 P.M.–1 A.M. Wed., Fri., and Sat.)—part club, part bowling alley with bar—has played a part in Louisville history since the late 1800s, but is currently in the midst of a re-birth. The club hosts shows by up-and-coming bands (check the online schedule), and The Vernon's eight bowling lanes are the coolest place in town to doff bowling shoes. For a change from the usual scene, The Vernon is your spot.

Sergio's World Beers (1605 Story Ave., 502/618-2337, www.sergiosworldbeers.com, 2 P.M.–midnight Mon.–Thurs. and Sun., 2 P.M.–2 A.M. Fri.–Sat.) is not the place to go

if you think that beer is beer. If, however, you are a discerning beer drinker, a connoisseur of the sudsy stuff, then you'll want to locate this discreet (there's no signage) temple to beer to surround yourself with like-minded individuals and get lost in the selection of 1,200 beers, over 40 of which are on tap. The place feels a bit like a private club, but as long as you hold a healthy amount of respect for the product on tap, you'll be welcomed by Sergio, who mans the bar himself. Bring cash as it's the only form of payment accepted.

Bardstown Road

Louisville's original nightlife center, Bardstown Road is still where many locals go to meet and mingle or just grab a stool at the neighborhood watering hole. Many a weekend gets kicked off at Louisville's Irish corner, located just past where Bardstown Road turns into Baxter Avenue and the home of **O'Shea's Traditional Irish Pub** (956 Baxter Ave., 502/589-7373, 11 A.M.–midnight Sun.–Thurs., 11 A.M.–4 A.M. Fri.–Sat.), **Flanagan's Ale House** (934 Baxter Ave., 502/585-3211, 11 A.M.–midnight Sun.–Thurs., 11 A.M.–4 A.M. Fri.–Sat.), and **Molly Malone's Irish Pub** (933 Baxter Ave., 502/473-1222, 11 A.M.–midnight

Sun.–Thurs., 11 A.M.–4 A.M. Fri.–Sat.). Molly's draws in a large college student contingency, while O'Shea's, with its three bars and two lovely courtyards, and Flanagan's, with more than 100 beers on tap, cater to a more mixed crowd. It's not unusual to find people hopping between all three.

If you're looking for a more chill atmosphere to enjoy some fine hometown suds, then slide into a booth at **Cumberland Brewery** (1576 Bardstown Rd., 502/458-8727, www.cumberlandbrewery.com, 4 P.M.–2 A.M. Mon.–Thurs., noon–2 A.M. Fri.–Sat., 1 P.M.–2 A.M. Sun.). Ten of their brews are on tap every day, and they routinely tap kegs of specialty beers. A well-received menu of pub grub staves off any hunger and complements their tasty selection of craft beer.

When the weather is nice, make **Monkey Wrench** (1025 Barrett Ave., 502/582-2433, 4 P.M.–2 A.M. Tues.–Fri., noon–2 A.M. Sat., 10 A.M.–2 A.M. Sun.) your destination. Located in a former Laundromat, this spacious bar has a fantastic rooftop deck where you can enjoy inexpensive drinks. A small cover may be charged if you opt to drink inside and enjoy the live music, but the deck is always free.

More interested in nightclubs than bars? Then **Phoenix Hill Tavern** (644 Baxter Ave., 502/589-4957, www.phoenixhill.com, 8 P.M.–4 A.M. Wed. and Sat., 8 P.M.–3 A.M. Thurs., 5 P.M.–4 A.M. Fri.) is your best bet. On weekends, live music plays from three stages, and in summer, the dance party moves outdoors to the deck. Phoenix Hill also hosts national acts and special events. Check the online calendar.

LIVE MUSIC
Downtown
Stevie Ray's Blues Bar (230 E. Main St., 502/582-9945, www.stevieraysbluesbar.com, 4 P.M.–midnight Mon.–Tues., 4 P.M.–1 A.M. Wed.–Thurs., 4 P.M.–3 A.M. Fri., 6 P.M.–3 A.M. Sat.) brings in some of the nation's best blues musicians as well as top local talent. Crowds regularly pack the bar, which is equally welcoming to those who like to enjoy their blues

with a drink at a table and those who feel the need to get up and dance.

In the basement of the Glassworks building, **Jazzyblu** (815 W. Market St., 502/992-3243, www.jazzyblu.com, 8 P.M.–2 A.M. Fri.–Sat.), appeals to the artsy crowd with its upscale lounge feel and its weekend music schedule. On Fridays, regional musicians perform styles ranging from blues to Latin, while Saturdays are focused on neo-soul music.

Bardstown Road
Highlands Tap Room (1279 Bardstown Rd., 502/459-2337, www.highlandstaproom.com, 4 P.M.–4 A.M. daily) offers live music seven days a week and never charges a cover. The music is diverse, ranging from rock and indie to blues and bluegrass, and bands are both local and regional. The bar also hosts open mic and karaoke nights. On busy nights, getting to the bar to order one of the 13 microbrews they have on tap can be difficult, but the crowd is friendly.

COMEDY CLUBS
Bardstown Road
Comedy Caravan (1250 Bardstown Rd., 502/459-0022, www.comedycaravan.com) has been making Louisville laugh for over two decades. Nationally known comedians share the stage with up-and-coming performers, all of whom know how to tell a joke or two. Shows are held at 8 P.M. and 10 P.M. on Wednesdays, Thursdays, and Sundays, at 8 P.M. and 10:30 P.M. on Fridays, and at 7:15 P.M., 9:30 P.M. and 11:45 P.M. on Saturdays. You must be 18 or older to attend. Reservations are recommended, or you can purchase tickets online for $2 less than at the box office.

MOVIE THEATERS
Bardstown Road
Louisville has plenty of theaters showing blockbuster hits and offering stadium seating. But if you're looking to catch a foreign or independent film, you want to get a ticket at **Baxter Avenue Theatre** (1250 Bardstown Rd., 502/456-4404, www.baxter8.com). Blockbuster films that border on the artistic

are also shown. Film freaks won't want to miss Midnight at the Baxter, a series in which cult classics appear in all their 35mm glory on the big screen every other Saturday.

East Louisville

For a cheap night out, screen a flick at **Village 8** (4014 Dutchmans Ln., 502/894-8697, www.village8.com), Louisville's discount theater. Tickets are only $4 in the evening, $3 before 6 P.M. Every Friday a new first-run independent, foreign, or art-house film opens at Village 8 as part of the Louisville Exclusive Film series.

PERFORMING ARTS
Kentucky Center for the Performing Arts

The stages of the Kentucky Center for the Performing Arts (501 W. Main St., 502/562-0100, www.kentuckycenter.org) are home to the talent of the Louisville Ballet, Louisville Orchestra, and Kentucky Opera, as well as the actors of the Broadway Across America series and the Stage One children's theater. The Center also puts on concerts, shows, and performances from non-resident groups and popular artists in a series called Kentucky Center Presents. With three stages on-site, ranging from the tiny experimental MeX, to the kid-friendly Bomhard, to the crowd-welcoming Whitney Hall, as well as the grand stage of the nearby Brown Theatre (315 W. Broadway), the Kentucky Center is where you go to see great performing art from every genre. All shows draw big crowds, but for the Broadway series in particular, be sure to get tickets well in advance, as the best seats for these shows sell out quickly.

Actor's Theatre

For powerful performances of both groundbreaking and classic plays, Actor's Theatre (316 W. Main St., 502/584-1205,

Kentucky Center for the Performing Arts

LOUISVILLE

www.actorstheatre.org) is the hottest act in town. The Tony Award–winning theater is known for its daring and innovation, introducing over 300 plays into the greater theater world and premiering three Pulitzer Prize winners. It's also known by locals for its annual production of *A Christmas Carol,* which seems to get better every year. The theater's three stages are reached through a magnificent lobby that was originally built as the imposing Bank of Louisville building in 1837.

Louisville Palace

When big-name comedians, musicians who like to provide their audience with an intimate experience, and other performers of national note come to town, you can usually find them at the Louisville Palace (625 4th Ave., 502/583-4555, www.louisvillepalace.com). This performing arts space lives up to its high-reaching name thanks to its many visual pleasures. Built in 1928, it cost $2 million—a remarkable amount then—and you'll understand why immediately. The Spanish Baroque design translates into a lobby of bright red, gold, and blue with a vaulted ceiling featuring carvings of such greats as Shakespeare and Beethoven. Entering the theater, you'll feel as though you've stepped into a Spanish courtyard thanks to the plethora of arcades, balconies, and turrets, and the ceiling painted like the midnight sky. Come for the show or come for the theater; either way you'll have an amazing experience.

ART GALLERIES

Art is thriving in the River City, with galleries popping up all around town. In fact, the gallery scene has exploded so much that two monthly hops are needed to keep patrons happy, though galleries are, of course, open outside of trolley hop hours.

◖ First Friday Trolley Hop

Since the most recent turn of the century, downtown Louisville's Main and Market Streets have transformed into the place to be for art lovers. Galleries abound, and thanks to the First Friday Trolley Hop

(www.firstfridaytrolleyhop.com), they're all easy to visit and welcoming to both the committed art patron as well as the casual browser. From 5 to 11 P.M. on the first Friday of each month, historic trolleys circulate through the art district, offering free rides between 27 art galleries, as well as the nearby restaurants and bars. Art galleries often hold exhibition openings on First Friday nights, while restaurants offer special menus and deals. A full listing of participating galleries with links to their individual websites can be found on the Trolley Hop website, so you can plan in advance where you want to stop. On First Fridays, most galleries stay open until 9 P.M. A few of the most popular galleries are listed here. Free parking is available at Slugger Field, the Fourth Street Live! parking garage, and on the street after 6 P.M.

Glassworks (815 W. Market St., 502/584-4510, www.louisvilleglassworks.com) is an arts facility unlike any other in the nation in that it combines three working glass studios with two galleries and then throws in workshop space to boot. Glassblowers, flameworkers, and architectural glass artists from throughout the U.S. seek opportunities to work at Glassworks, and on a self-guided (10 A.M.–4 P.M. Mon.–Fri., $4.50 adults, $3.50 seniors and students) or guided tour (11 A.M., 1 P.M., 3 P.M. Sat., $6.50 adults, $5.50 seniors, $4.50 students), you can watch the artists work their magic. Items ranging from earrings to dining tables, all made of glass, are available for purchase. For those looking to dive into the world of glass, instruction options include walk-in workshops, "blow your own" events, and classes.

Glass art thrives in community settings, as proven by Seattle and other glass hot spots, so it's not surprising that Glassworks isn't the only act in town. Nearby **Flame Run** (828 E. Market St., 502/584-5353, www.flamerun.org, 10 A.M.–4 P.M., Tues.–Sat.) actually has the biggest glass blowing studio in the region and plays host to an array of exhibitions. Classes are also on offer.

If you're looking for fine art, **Zephyr Gallery** (601 E. Market St., 502/585-5646, www.zephyrgallery.org, 11 A.M.–6 P.M. Wed.–Sat.) is a cooperative gallery with 24 members who show their work on a rotating basis. **Pyro Gallery** (624 W. Main St., 502/587-0106, www.pyrogallery.com, 11 A.M.–3 P.M. Thurs. and Sun., 11 A.M.–5 P.M. Fri.–Sat.) seeks to ignite, excite, and inspire visitors through its exhibitions, which feature the work of the gallery's cooperative members, both well-known and emerging local artists specializing in a variety of art forms.

F.A.T. Friday Hop

Trolley hop fun isn't limited to the first Friday of the month; it's also scheduled for 6–10:30 P.M. on the last Friday of the month, when the beloved TARC trolley makes its way to Frankfort Avenue for the F.A.T. Friday Hop, offering free rides to hop participants. Though the Frankfort Avenue area boasts less art galleries than downtown, it makes up for it with its awesome collection of boutiques, specialty shops, and restaurants. Find a descriptive list of all participants on the F.A.T. Friday website. For the art lover, galleries of interest are mentioned here. Most stay open until 9 P.M. on F.A.T. Fridays.

Revitalizing and renovating old and abandoned spaces has caught on big in Louisville, and a fine example of a successful effort is the conversion of the former Fischer Meat Packing Plant into the current **Mellwood Arts & Entertainment Center** (1860 Mellwood Ave., 502/895-3650, www.mellwoodartscenter.com). The 360,000-square-foot industrial building now houses over 180 artist studios, as well as galleries, retail stores, and event space. It's easy to get lost in the labyrinth of studios, but that's half the fun since you'll discover exciting artwork around each corner. You can often see artists in action, and many are happy to discuss their work with you. If the genre exists, you'll find it at Mellwood. Though the center is open 9 A.M.–9 P.M. daily, not all artists are there at all times. For the best chance of finding the artist you're looking for in studio, visit during the trolley hop or during market hours (11 A.M.–4 P.M. Wed.–Sat.).

At **Pottery Rowe** (2048 Frankfort Ave., 502/896-0877, www.potteryrowe.com, 10 A.M.–5 P.M. Mon.–Sat.), a combo studio and showroom, every dish, every ornament, every vase—let's just say every everything—on sale is created by hand by owner Melvin Rowe. You'll probably see him when you enter, working at his wheel to the tunes of country music. He'll happily chat with you about his work and then leave you to explore on your own. Though every pot takes three weeks to complete, prices are more than reasonable, and it's hard to leave empty-handed.

If you're a fan of forged iron and bronze sculpture and furniture, check out **Kaviar Forge & Gallery** (147 Stevenson Ave., 502/561-0377, www.craigkaviar.com, noon–6 P.M. Wed.–Fri., noon–4 P.M. Sat.), where artist Craig Kaviar turns out award-winning forged work. He offers his creations, as well as paintings and ceramics by other artists, in a gallery, from which visitors can peer through a window to watch him at work.

FESTIVALS AND EVENTS

Not a month goes by in Louisville without a festival. There are festivals to celebrate ethnic food, festivals to celebrate music, festivals to celebrate major holidays, and festivals to celebrate minor holidays. Open a city paper to the events page, and you're sure to find a long listing of festivals and events. It's more than any one human could ever attend in a year, but go ahead and give it a try. If you fail, you won't be the first. Just be sure that no matter what life throws your way, you make it to the following big-time events.

◖ Kentucky Derby Festival

The Kentucky Derby might be known as the most exciting two minutes in sports, but to Louisville, the Derby lasts far longer than two minutes. In fact, thanks to the Kentucky Derby Festival (www.kdf.org), Derby excitement lasts for a complete two weeks.

The party kicks off on the Saturday exactly two weeks before the Derby (which is always the first Saturday in May) with **Thunder Over**

Louisville, the largest annual fireworks display in the world. For nearly 30 minutes, eight 400-foot barges anchored in the Ohio River around the Second Street Bridge shoot a barrage of pyrotechnics into the night, turning Louisville's downtown sky into an explosion of color. Crowning the show is the mile-long waterfall of fireworks that cascades down from the bridge. The celebration begins long before dark, however, with an air show that lifts off in mid-afternoon and features performances by skydive and aeronautic teams as well as flyovers by military jets. The best viewing spots are at Waterfront Park. Claim yours early.

Next on the agenda for most Derby Festival attendees is the **Great BalloonFest,** which takes place the weekend after Thunder, stretching from Thursday through Saturday. The headliner events are Friday's Great Balloon Glow and Saturday's Great Balloon Race. On Friday night at 9 P.M. at the Kentucky Exposition Center (937 Phillips Ln., 502/367-5000, www.kyfairexpo.org), the nearly 50 balloons scheduled to participate in the next morning's race are inflated but not launched. As the pilots fire their burners, the balloons glow against the black sky, creating a truly magical sight. Observers are invited to walk among the glowing balloons and chat with the pilots. Just a brief sleep later, at around 7 A.M. Saturday morning, the hot air balloons lift off from the same spot and brighten the skies of Louisville as they fight to win the race. In order to do so, the chase balloons must follow a hare balloon (usually the previous year's winner), which chooses a landing spot where a large target is set up. The winning balloon is the one that is able to get a bag of bluegrass seed nearest to the target by dropping it from their balloon. It's harder than it sounds. A Balloon Glimmer at Waterfront Park, a Balloon Rush Hour Race, and a Balloon Tour round out the BalloonFest. More information on each event is available on the Kentucky Derby Festival website. All balloon events are weather permitting.

Also taking place on the Saturday one week before Derby Day is the **Derby Festival Marathon and Mini-Marathon.** The starter gun fires at 7:30 A.M., with runners taking off from Southern Parkway and heading toward Iroquois Park. Racers then head north for a lap around Churchill Downs and a foray into downtown. Those running the 13.1-mile mini finish there, while marathoners head east to loop through Cherokee Park, then cross over into Southern Indiana, before also finishing downtown. If you're not a runner, join one of the organized cheering sections, or just find a spot on the sidewalk to propel the racers forward with your support.

During Derby week, the Festival really heats up, with the end of the week especially loaded with popular events. Wednesday evening you'll want to make your way to the Waterfront for the **Great Steamboat Race** (6 P.M.), which pits the hometown *Belle of Louisville* against an out-of-town competitor. For decades, the *Delta Queen* was the *Belle*'s arch nemesis, but due to the *Delta Queen*'s legal problems, the *Belle of Cincinnati* has taken her place. The two boats race a course down the Ohio River and back to port, but recent changes to the rules mean that the first boat across the finish line isn't necessarily the winner of the coveted gilded antlers. Instead the winner is the boat that accumulates the most points in a competition involving five pre-designated tasks, one being a calliope-playing contest. If you're not content to watch the race from shore, you can purchase a dinner cruise ticket for either boat.

On Thursday afternoon at 5 P.M., the Festival's original event, the **Pegasus Parade,** gets underway. Broadway, from Campbell Street to 9th Street, is taken over by floats, marching bands, equestrian units, celebrities, clowns, and inflatables, and cheering crowds cram the sidewalks. Tickets are available for bleacher seats ($9) and chairs ($11), but most people just bring their own blankets and lawn chairs and claim a street-side spot. If you're a true parade aficionado, get an in-depth look at the floats and performers during the Parade Preview, which takes place on the Tuesday evening before the race at the Kentucky Exposition Center.

© THERESA DOWELL BLACKINTON

Pegasus Parade

As much as Louisville loves fireworks, balloons, and parades, by Friday of Derby week all thoughts have turned to horse racing. Though the big event is still a day away, you'll find Churchill Downs nearly as packed. Locals, who often spend Derby Day itself at parties rather than at the track, flock to Churchill Downs for the running of the **Kentucky Oaks,** a premiere race for fillies established alongside the Derby in 1875. As with the Derby, the infield is open for the full day of racing, and attendance routinely tops 100,000. The scene is a bit more laid-back than on Derby Day, making it a favorite for families. General admission tickets, which allow you entrance to the infield and first-floor paddock, are $25 and available at the gate. Reserved seats must be purchased in conjunction with Derby tickets. After the races, one final pre-Derby event takes place: the **Barnstable Brown Party,** a Derby Eve gala attended by celebrities of every stripe. Legions of fans line up outside the home of Patricia Barnstable Brown (1700 Spring Dr.) in the hopes of spotting their favorite stars.

The denouement of all the celebrating, and the reason the Festival takes place at all, is the **Kentucky Derby,** run every year since 1875 at Churchill Downs, making it the longest running sporting event in the United States. Though the actual Run for the Roses is the 10th race of the day, with the traditional singing of *My Old Kentucky Home* and the call to the post taking place around 6 P.M., the gates at Churchill Downs open at 8 A.M., and the racing starts at 11 A.M. Join the over 150,000 people who attend the Derby each year for an experience everyone should have at least once. In the grandstands, women wear extravagant hats, men wear seersucker suits, and everyone enjoys at least one mint julep. When it's time to watch the best three-year-old thoroughbreds in the nation race, all eyes turn to the track. Overhead in Millionaire's Row, Hollywood celebrities air kiss each other and pose for the camera in designer outfits. And in the 40 acres of infield, where most Derby attendees end up, anything goes. Though you can catch a glimpse of the horses passing by if you push your way up to the fence and you can see all the races on the infield's big-screen TVs, most people come to the infield to party rather than watch the horses run. The area near the third turn is particularly notorious for its raucous behavior, which almost always involves alcohol snuck in via ingenious methods and frequently involves mud, nudity, and other behavior that your parents would not approve of. But don't fear, if that's not your scene, just head toward the first turn, where families tend to congregate and even Miss Manners would find little to shake her head at. General admission tickets cost $40 and an unlimited number are available at the gate. Without a lot of money or luck, obtaining reserved seats for the Derby is nearly impossible. Tickets for the Derby and Oaks are sold together in a package. You can submit a ticket request to Churchill Downs via their website (www.churchilldowns.com), which will enter you into a lottery for tickets. Additionally, a few thousand tickets are released for public sale, again via the website, in December or January. These tickets range in price from $172 for a grandstand bleacher seat to $6,390 for a six-seat box in the third-floor clubhouse.

Aside from the Oaks and Derby, all events mentioned here are free to spectators with a Derby pin. Pins can be purchased at the entrance to all events for $5, as well as at local grocery stores, drugstores, and other retailers for $4. The Kentucky Derby Festival consists of many more events than those outlined here, so check the website for a full calendar of events with descriptions.

Humana Festival of New American Plays

Be the first to know what's the next hot thing in theater by attending the annual Humana Festival of New American Plays (www.actorstheatre.org/humana.htm). This internationally renowned festival, held for seven consecutive weeks between February and April, unveils the best new works by American playwrights. Many of these plays have gone on to win prestigious prizes. The excitement in the air is palpable. For theater buffs, attending the festival is a must. In addition to single performance tickets, packages are also available.

Forecastle Festival

Billing itself as a music/art/activism festival, the Forecastle Festival (http://forecastlefest.com) is a huge three-day outdoor concert with side shows focusing on art and environmental awareness. The festival, which is held at Waterfront Park in early July, features over 100 bands and is considered one of the premier outdoor events in the nation. In 2010, performers included the Smashing Pumpkins, the Flaming Lips, Widespread Panic, Cake, Drive-By Truckers, Modern English, Dar Williams, and a slew of other artists from a wide variety of genres. For many attendees, the event is as much about the experience as the music. Single-day and three-day tickets are available.

Abbey Road on the River

Though you might assume the world's largest Beatles music festival would be held in England, you'd be wrong. It's actually held in Louisville over Memorial Day weekend. At Abbey Road on the River (www.abbeyroadontheriver.com), over 60 bands pay tribute to the Beatles during five days of rocking and rolling at the waterfront Belvedere Park. When the official partying ends around 1 A.M., many attendees head to the nearby Galt House for sing-a-longs of Beatles favorites. The hotel also hosts film viewings as well as a few indoor stages. If you can't get enough of John, Paul, George, and Ringo, you won't want to miss this festival. Five-day tickets offer the best value, but you can also buy single-day tickets.

Kentucky Shakespeare Festival

Every summer from mid-June to mid-July, the Kentucky Shakespeare Festival (www.kyshakes.org) raises the curtain on the stage at the C. Douglas Ramsey Amphitheatre in Old Louisville's Central Park and presents two or three of the Bard's works. No matter what plays they're putting on, expect elaborate costumes, impressive scenery, and accomplished actors. Dating back to 1949, making it the oldest free and independent Shakespeare festival in the United States, Shakespeare in Central Park is a Louisville tradition and draws big crowds. The amphitheater can seat 1,000 people, but you're also welcome to view your "Free Will" from a blanket on the lawn. Bring a picnic to enjoy before the 8 P.M. show and make it an evening.

Kentucky State Fair

The Kentucky State Fair (Kentucky Exposition Center, 937 Phillips Ln., www.kystatefair.org), occupying an 11-day stretch of late August every year, is an end-of-summer rite. From fine-arts competitions to tobacco judging, from livestock shows to beauty pageants, from the thrill of pig races to the suspense of the pipe-smoking contest, the Kentucky State Fair offers something for everyone. A huge midway, as well as a series of free and ticketed concerts, rounds out the offerings. Admire the skill of quilters, judge for yourself which goat deserves a blue ribbon, pick up as many freebies as you can carry, say hello to giant Freddy Farm Bureau, or just people-watch. To fit it all in, you'll need a few days, especially if you want to take in events such as the World Championship Horse Show. You'll also want to come hungry as there's a feast of food to be had. For a real taste of the Bluegrass State, forego the carnival classic corndog and gyro stands and instead visit the Kentucky Proud Tent for your choice of locally produced treats. The pork chop sandwiches are hard to beat. Tickets are available at the gate. Before the Fair begins, discounted tickets are available at area Kroger grocery stores.

St. James Court Art Show

Fine art and fine homes go well together, which may explain why the St. James Court Art Show (Old Louisville, www.stjamescourtartshow.com, 10 A.M.–6 P.M. Fri.–Sat., 10 A.M.–5 P.M. Sun., free), which takes place in the heart of Old Louisville on the first full weekend in October, is such a well-attended event. Consistently ranked by artists and art organizations as one of the top art shows in the nation, St. James features 750 artists from across the continent. At booths set up amidst the mansions on St. James and Belgravia Courts as well as on Magnolia, 3rd, and 4th Streets, you'll find works in 16 mediums, ranging from fiber to clay to metal to wood to photography, and in price ranges to fit any and all budgets. Artists are chosen through a competitive selection process, and all work is juried.

Shopping

SHOPPING DISTRICTS

Like every mid-size city in the United States, Louisville has its share of shopping malls and big box stores, but what causes even the most reformed shopaholic to fall off the wagon is Louisville's abundance of boutiques. From designer label clothes to duds designed by the next Project Runway star, from bookshops with personality to music shops that never stop jamming, Louisville's got it, and to make shopping simple, it's all conveniently located in two main shopping districts.

Frankfort Avenue

Frankfort Avenue has, in the years since a new century rolled in, resumed its historic role as a central area for local business and blossomed into Louisville's fashion destination. Leading the way stylistically is the mixed-use Lodge 820, with four of its ground floor shops dedicated to high fashion. **Peacock Boutique** (2828 Frankfort Ave., 502/897-1158, www.shopthepeacock.com, 10 A.M.–7 P.M. Mon.–Sat., noon–5 P.M. Sun.) and the **Dressing Room** (2836 Frankfort Ave., 502/896-8733,

11 A.M.–5 P.M. Mon., Fri., and Sat., 11 A.M.–6 P.M. Tues.–Thurs.) are where Louisville's best dressed go when they need to make an impression. Both shops specialize in the latest styles from top designers and offer personalized service. The designer shoes and handbags on offer at **Stiletto Boutique** (2846 Frankfort Ave., 502/614-8130, www. stilettoboutique.net, 10 A.M.–6 P.M. Tues.–Sat.) and the handmade jewelry fashioned by designer Gayle Andres at **Honeysuckle Moon** (2842 Frankfort Ave., 502/523-9209, 10 A.M.–5 P.M. Tues.–Fri., 10 A.M.–4 P.M. Sat.) complete any outfit.

For those with expensive taste but a smaller budget, you don't have to leave Frankfort Avenue empty handed. A number of high-end consignment shops, some featuring never-worn clothes and styles that you can still find on other stores' full-price racks, are located on Frankfort Avenue. For the best chance of walking away with a designer outfit at a bargain price, make your way to **Margaret's Consignment** (2700 Frankfort Ave., 502/896-4706, 10 A.M.–5 P.M. Mon.–Sat., noon–4 P.M. Sun.) and **Urban Kitty** (2638 Frankfort Ave., 502/893-1950, 11 A.M.–6 P.M. Wed.–Sat.). If vintage is more your style, pop into **Elizabeth's Timeless Attire** (2050 Frankfort Ave., 502/895-5911, noon–6 P.M. Tues.–Sat.) to dress yourself and then **2023** (2023 Frankfort Ave., 502/899-9872, 11 A.M.–5 P.M. Tues.–Sat.) to dress your home.

There's more to Frankfort Avenue than fashion, however. While you're out strolling this pedestrian-friendly corridor, take time to browse at these other Frankfort Avenue favorites: **Quest Outdoors** (2330 Frankfort Ave., 502/893-5746, www. questoutdoors.com, 10 A.M.–8 P.M. Mon.–Fri., 10 A.M.–6 P.M. Sat., noon–5 P.M. Sun.), Louisville's local answer to REI; **Just Creations** (2722 Frankfort Ave., 502/897-7319, www.justcreations.org, 10 A.M.–6 P.M. Mon.–Sat.), a not-for-profit, fair-trade shop featuring products from 35 developing nations in Asia, Africa, Central America, and South America; and **The Wine Rack** (2632

Frankfort Ave., 502/721-9148, www.thewinerack.us, 10 A.M.–9 P.M. Mon.–Thurs., 10 A.M.–10 P.M. Fri.–Sat., 1–5 P.M. Sun.), where the "10 for around $10" offerings make fine wine accessible to everyone.

Bardstown Road

The Highlands is a true Louisville original, a neighborhood chock full of beautiful houses and local shops, bars, and restaurants, and Bardstown Road is the epicenter of it all. For shoppers, the one-mile stretch between Eastern Parkway and Baxter Avenue is paradise. So park your car, put on your walking (but still stylish) shoes, and explore. It's a bustling area, where you'll see couples and families, hipsters and preps, punks and preachers all promenading down the sidewalks. Join them in window browsing at the welcoming storefronts, and then go ahead and pop in a shop when something catches your eye. If you need structure to your shopping, here are a few suggestions.

If you're looking for an original Louisville souvenir, such as a t-shirt that you won't find anywhere else, drop in at **WHY Louisville** (1583 Bardstown Rd., 502/456-5400, www. whylouisville.com, 10 A.M.–9 P.M. Mon.–Fri., 9 A.M.–9 P.M. Sat., 11 A.M.–7 P.M. Sun.), where all the goods are made by local and regional designers. You can also find cool, although not local, t-shirts at nearby **Dot Fox** (1567 Bardstown Rd., 502/452-9191, www.dotfox-clothingculture.com, 11 A.M.–8 P.M. Mon.–Thurs., 11 A.M.–9 P.M. Fri.–Sat., noon–6 P.M. Sun.), a local take on Urban Outfitters where trendy clothing is sold alongside kitsch. For more fashion fun, head down the street to **General Eccentric** (1600 Bardstown Rd., 502/458-8111, www.generaleccentric.com, 11 A.M.–8 P.M. Mon.–Thurs., 11 A.M.–9 P.M. Fri.–Sat., noon–6 P.M. Sun.), where you can always find the latest trends, though if you like it you better buy it, since they stock limited quantities of each style. You wouldn't want to be caught dead in the same outfit as someone else, now would you? To complete your outfit, run across the street to

Leatherhead (1601 Bardstown Rd., 502/451-4477, www.theleatherhead.com, 11:30 A.M.–7:30 P.M. Mon.–Fri., 11 A.M.–5 P.M. Sat.), where they'll custom design you a belt or bag if none of the in-stock pieces suit you. Another great place to accessorize is **Luna Boutique** (1310 Bardstown Rd., 502/454-7620, www.lunaboutique.net, 10 A.M.–6 P.M. Mon.–Sat.), where you'll find a fantastic selection of jewelry, handbags, and hats.

Fashion isn't all that's on sale on Bardstown Road. **Carmichael's** (1295 Bardstown Rd., 502/456-6950, www.carmichaelsbookstore.com, 8 A.M.–10 P.M. Sun.–Thurs., 8 A.M.–11 P.M. Fri.–Sat.) is Louisville's favorite bookstore, winning over customers with its book-loving sales staff, its hand-picked collection, and its neighborhood feel. You won't find every book ever written here, but you will find every book worth reading. The music equivalent of Carmichael's is **Ear X-Tacy** (2226 Bardstown Rd., 502/459-8130, www.earx-tacy.com, 10 A.M.–10 P.M. Mon.–Sat., noon–8 P.M. Sun.), which faced closure in 2010 but rallied to stay open thanks to the support of the local community and a move to a smaller store. With an all-knowing staff and awesome collections of music running the gamut from mainstream to the band you've never heard of but have to hear, Ear X-Tacy is a destination for music lovers.

ARTS AND CRAFTS

Since 1815, **Louisville Stoneware** (731 Brent St., 502/582-1900, www.louisvillestoneware.com, 10 A.M.–6 P.M. Mon.–Sat.) has been providing the Derby City with original dinnerware and house decor. The stoneware—designed, fired, and painted at the Brent Street studio—comes in a variety of motifs and colors, both traditional and modern. The mint julep cups, Hot Brown trays, and Kentucky Pie plates make great souvenirs, and the Equine and Fleur De Lis patterns are very popular. If you'd like to see the stoneware being created, visit at 10:30 A.M. or 1:30 P.M., when studio tours are offered for $7. If none of the designs suit your fancy, then you're welcome to paint

your own stoneware. The $25 paint-your-own price includes a tour.

Though it has a shorter history than Louisville Stoneware—dating back to 1940—**Hadley Pottery** (1570 Story Ave., 502/584-2171, www.hadleypottery.com, 8 A.M.–5 P.M. Mon.–Fri., 9 A.M.–1 P.M. Sat.) is also a well-loved local institution. The "Hadley blue" paint appearing on all the pottery is instantly recognizable, and the whimsical designs, originally created by Mary Alice Hadley and now painted by her protégées, hold a strong fan base. The holiday plates make for fun collector's items, and kids in particular love the animal designs. Many of the items can be personalized. Hadley Pottery is sold throughout the country, but the factory in Louisville is where it's all created, and you're welcome to tour the Pottery as well as browse the showroom.

ANTIQUES

Comb through the two acres of treasures at **Joe Ley Antiques** (615 E. Market St., 502/583-4014, www.joeley.com, 8:30 A.M.–5 P.M. Tues.–Sat.), and you're sure to find something you just have to have. Whether you're in search of a new mantle for an old house, antique furniture, a Tiffany light fixture, or something as unique as a carousel horse, you'll find it at Joe Ley. Even if you have no intent to buy, it's still a fun place to browse, a bit like a trip into grandma's attic.

LOCAL PRODUCTS

If you're unable to hit all of the local sites and shops but need to get gifts and souvenirs, then head to **A Taste of Kentucky** (Mall St. Matthews, 5000 Shelbyville Rd., 502/895-2733, www.atasteofkentucky.com, 10 A.M.–9 P.M. Mon.–Sat., noon–6 P.M. Sun.). It's where locals go when they want to give a gift that is as authentic as bluegrass. Items come from all over the city and state, and include artwork, food, drink, books, Derby memorabilia, and more. The store even offers pre-made gift baskets that provide a sampler of Kentucky bests.

LOUISVILLE

MALLS

Louisville's top malls are located directly next to each other. **Mall St. Matthews** (5000 Shelbyville Rd., 502/893-0311, www.mallstmatthews.com) is anchored by Dillards and J. C. Penney, while **Oxmoor Center** (7900 Shelbyville Rd., 502/426-3000, www.oxmoorcenter.com) is anchored by Sears, Macy's, and Von Maur. Between the two of them, you should be able to find just about anything.

Sports and Recreation

PARKS

There are 124 city parks that dot Louisville (18 of them in the Olmsted System), so no matter where you are, there's a park nearby. To find the one that most suits your interests, visit the Metro Parks website (http://louisvilleky.gov/metroparks) and use the Park Finder, which allows you to search by name, location, or park amenities.

◖ Olmsted Park System

Though landscape architect Frederick Law Olmsted is probably best known for New York's Central Park, many critics consider the park system he designed for Louisville to be his greatest accomplishment. Locals certainly think so. Consisting of three large flagship parks—Cherokee, Iroquois, and Shawnee—connected by six tree-lined parkways, with fifteen smaller parks and playgrounds along the way, Louisville's Olmsted Park System (www.olmstedparks.org) is where Louisvillians go for a breath of fresh air.

CHEROKEE PARK

Cherokee Park (Willow Ave. and Cherokee Pkwy.) is the most popular park in the city, drawing nearly 500,000 visitors annually. In the Beargrass Creek Valley, Cherokee's 409 acres boast wide open spaces perfect for picnics and pick-up games and broad vistas that reward hikers, joggers, and bikers. The always busy 2.4-mile Scenic Loop is a mixed-use, one-way road, with one lane for cars and another dedicated to person-powered transport. Other favorite areas include the sport-lover's Frisbee Field, the dog run at Cochran Hill, the playground at Hogan's Fountain, and the eternal hangout of Big Rock. The park also sports an archery range, bird sanctuary, nine-hole golf course, and a series of trails shared by hikers and mountain bikers. Thanks to Cherokee Park's many entrances and exits, even locals are known to get confused when driving through, so it's best to consult the park and trail maps online to plan your outing.

IROQUOIS PARK

The southern anchor of the Olmsted Park System, Iroquois Park (Southern Pkwy. and Taylor Blvd.) is known for its rugged terrain and the over 10,000-year-old forest that constitutes the heart of the park. From the park summit, home to one of many outlooks that dot Iroquois's 739 acres, visitors can take in a grand panorama of Louisville. Take a bike up to the summit for a challenge, or test your athletic prowess on the basketball courts, disc golf course, or 18-hole golf course. The Iroquois amphitheater, home to warm-weather productions and concerts, is another highlight of the park.

SHAWNEE PARK

Shawnee Park (Southwestern Pkwy. and Broadway), in western Louisville, makes the most of its riverfront setting with a Great Lawn popular for family reunions and other large gatherings. The basketball courts, baseball fields, and tennis courts are often busy, and the 18-hole golf course is the only city park course to offer a complete driving range facility. The 6.9-mile Riverwalk runs through Shawnee, and you can take it east to downtown's Waterfront Park or south to neighboring Chickasaw Park.

Waterfront Park

Encompassing 85 acres of riverfront real estate in downtown Louisville, Waterfront Park (www.louisvillewaterfront.com, 6 A.M.–11 P.M. daily) is home to most of the city's outdoor celebrations. Huge crowds gather on the Great Lawn and its surrounding green spaces for Thunder Over Louisville, the kick-off to the Derby Festival, as well as the Waterfront Independence Festival, a celebration of music and fireworks every July 3 and 4. The park also hosts numerous smaller festivals, concerts, and fundraiser walk/runs. In the summer, outdoor yoga classes and **Waterfront Wednesday,** a free after-work concert series scheduled for the last Wednesday of each month, are popular with downtown workers and visitors. Visit the park's website for a complete listing of the many events held here each year.

It doesn't take a festival, however, for the park to be bustling. It's a prime spot for a picnic, a bike ride, a walk, or a pick-up game of ultimate Frisbee or touch football. For kids, the playground and waterplay areas, complete with fountains you're invited to run through, are

the biggest draw. Recent additions to the park include a Lincoln Memorial, which celebrates Abe's connections to the state, and the Big 4 Pedestrian and Bicycling Bridge, which connects the Louisville waterfront with Southern Indiana. Parking is available on the street and in lots, most of which are free, along River Road.

Starting at the Belvedere in Waterfront Park is the 6.9-mile foot and bike path named the **Riverwalk** that runs along the Ohio River to Chickasaw Park in West Louisville. From there, another path picks up and leads you all the way to the Farnsley-Moremen Landing in southwest Louisville. These 25 miles of pathway make up the initial sections of the **Louisville Loop,** an in-the-works project that will result in a 110-mile paved bike and pedestrian trail circling the city, connecting parks and neighborhoods, and adding green space.

Louisville Extreme Park

Tony Hawk has named the Louisville Extreme Park (Clay St. and Franklin St., www.louisville-extremepark.org, 6 A.M.–11 P.M. daily) one of

fountains at Waterfront Park

Louisville Extreme Park

© MATTHEW DOWELL

© THERESA DOWELL BLACKINTON

his top five skate parks, so you know it's got to be good. The park's features—a 24-foot pipe, seven bowls ranging from 4 to 11 feet, a 12-foot wooden vertical ramp, and plenty of ledges and rails—invite skateboarders, in-line skaters, and bikers to show off their best moves. A rating system similar to that used on ski slopes identifies areas suitable for those with beginner, intermediate, and advanced-level skills. Don't forget your helmet as a local ordinance requires they be worn by all park users.

E. P. "Tom" Sawyer State Park

The only state park in Louisville, E. P. "Tom" Sawyer State Park (3000 Freys Hill Rd., 502/429-7270, http://parks.ky.gov, daylight–dark, free) doesn't lack for anything. Among its more standard offerings are a basketball and badminton gym, 12 tennis courts, a plethora of fields (14 soccer, 5 lacrosse, 3 softball, and 1 rugby), fitness and nature trails, and picnic shelters. A number of leagues use these facilities, and information about joining one can be found on the park's website. The park's less common features include a model airplane airfield, an archery range, and a BMX track (Mar.–Oct.). A four-acre dog park welcomes canines and their companions, and an Olympic-size pool (noon–6:30 P.M. Sun.–Fri., 10 A.M.–6:30 P.M. Sat. Memorial Day weekend–Labor Day, $4 ages 6 and up, $3 ages 3–5) is a park favorite. For a unique treat, take part in one of the monthly Star Parties sponsored by the Louisville Astronomical Society and held at the park (www.louisville-astro.org).

HIKING

Covering a remarkable 6,218 acres, **Jefferson Memorial Forest** (11311 Mitchell Hill Rd., 502/368-5404, www.memorialforest.com, 8 A.M.–dusk daily) is the largest municipal urban forest in the United States. Hikers in particular love this park, as it offers over 35 miles of trails. The longest and most challenging of these is the 6.2-mile, one-way Siltstone Trail, while the 0.2-mile Tuliptree Trail is the shortest and easiest. (It's also wheelchair accessible.) In between these two are a multitude of one-way and loop trails offering hikes of varying degrees of difficulty. Whichever you chose, you'll get to enjoy the bountiful plant life—50 types of trees and 17 species of ferns—as well as wildlife not often found in an urban setting—bobcats, coyotes, red foxes, white-tailed deer, great blue herons, and horned owls. For bird-watchers, a bird blind is available by appointment.

GOLF
Louisville Metro Parks

Nine of Louisville's Metro Parks feature public golf courses (http://louisvilleky.gov/MetroParks/golf), with six of these offering a full 18 holes. Varying in difficulty, the courses invite golfers of all abilities to play at affordable prices. Of the nine courses, the two most popular are **Seneca Golf Course** (2300 Pee Wee Reese Rd., 502/458-9298) and **Charlie Vettiner Golf Course** (10207 Mary Dell Ln., 502/267-9958). Seneca, with its hilly par-72 course running aside Beargrass Creek, has been ranked the sixth most difficult course in the state, while Charlie Vettiner, with 50 sand traps and three ponds, is ranked right behind Seneca as the seventh most challenging.

Quail Chase

Boasting country club standards without the membership fees, Quail Chase (7000 Cooper Chapel Rd., 502/239-5632, www.quailchase.com) is a public golf course with 27 championship regulation holes. Water hazards, bunkers, and tree-lined fairways make every round a challenge.

Valhalla

The premier golf course in Louisville, Valhalla (15503 Shelbyville Rd., 502/245-4475, www.valhalla.pgalinks.com) is a private club that has twice hosted the PGA Championship and most recently hosted the 2008 Ryder Cup. Valhalla is partially owned by the PGA and considered a difficult course by even the world's best golfers. Additional professional events are in the works, so check the website for information if you're interested in being a spectator. If you're a top-notch golfer and want to give the course a go yourself, you'll need to be the guest of a member or arrange guest privileges through the club.

SWIMMING

The **Mary T. Meagher Aquatic Center** (201 Reservoir Ave., 502/897-9949, http://louis-villeky.gov/MetroParks), named for Louisville's own Olympic champion, features an indoor Olympic-size pool open year-round for both exercise and recreational swimming. The pool is open 5 A.M.–9 P.M. Monday–Friday and 9 A.M.–6 P.M. on Saturdays, but recreational swim is restricted to noon–3:30 P.M. Monday–Friday with the addition of a 7–9 P.M. timeslot on Friday, and noon–6 P.M. on Saturday. Swim lessons, exercise classes, and lifeguarding classes are offered at the center. A day pass costs $4.50 for those over age 13, while those 12 and under pay $2.25. For frequent users, a membership is the best option.

BIKING

Bike Louisville is an effort of the city government to encourage biking. To map a route, find roads with bike lanes, connect to local bike organizations, or find a bike shop, visit http://louisvilleky.gov/bikelouisville. Among the most popular places for road biking in the city are Cherokee and Iroquois Parks and Jefferson Memorial Forest. Mountain bikers also like Cherokee and Iroquois, while BMX bikers stake claim to E. P. "Tom" Sawyer State Park.

Bike Clubs

The **Louisville Bicycle Club** (www.louis-villebicycleclub.org) organizes rides and events and advocates for cyclists. If you're looking for a group to ride with, check the calendar on their website, as they have rides scheduled nearly every day except Fridays. The LBC also sponsors the annual **Old Kentucky Home Tour,** a two-day ride with route options of 50, 72, and 102 miles. The century route takes riders all the way from E. P. "Tom" Sawyer State Park to Bardstown, Kentucky, where they overnight before returning the next day.

Bike Shops and Rentals

For all your biking needs, visit **Bardstown Road Bicycle Co.** (1051 Bardstown Rd., 502/485-9795, www.bardstownroadbi-cycles.com, 10 A.M.–7 P.M. Mon.–Wed., 10 A.M.–5 P.M. Thurs.–Sat.), where the knowledgeable staff can help you pick out a new bike, fix up an old bike, or gear up for any type of bike adventure.

At **Wheel Fun Rentals** (Waterfront Park, www.wheelfunrentals.com, 3 P.M.–dusk Fri., 10 A.M.–dusk Sat.–Sun.) you can rent a bicycle and explore Louisville's downtown and waterfront. Bikes available for rental range from your standard cruiser to tandem bikes to a double surrey that can transport your entire family. Guided tours are also available, departing on Saturdays at 10 A.M. and costing $25.

HORSEBACK RIDING

McNeely Lake Park Riding Stables (6711 Mount Washington Rd., 502/224-1469, www.louisvilleky.gov/MetroParks, daily) offers horseback riding in addition to lessons. Costs range from $20 for a 30-minute ride to $40 for a two-hour ride. These aren't thoroughbreds and this isn't the Derby, so no experience is necessary to enjoy a ride along the lakeside trails. Reservations are suggested.

SPECTATOR SPORTS
Horse Racing

Under the iconic spires of **Churchill Downs** (700 Central Ave., 502/636-4400, www.churchilldowns.com, $3 general admission), the world-famous Kentucky Derby is run every year on the first Saturday of May. The racetrack also hosts spring (late April–early July) and fall (late October–November) meets, where you can experience a full day of thoroughbred racing on both dirt and turf at the historic track. Pick up a program, wander over to the paddock for an up-close look at the contenders and their jockeys, place a bet, and then hurry down to the rail to cheer your pick on to the finish line. It's a classic way to pass a day in the Derby City. For a twist on traditional horse racing, check out Downs After

WIN, PLACE, OR SHOW:
HOW TO PLACE A BET AT CHURCHILL DOWNS

First, get a program. You're going to need to know what horses are racing, and you might want to know what jockey is onboard what horse, what the horses previous race results are, or maybe just what color silks the jockeys will be wearing. We all have different methods for picking a winner.

Second, scan the tote board to see the current odds for each horse. They change continually as people place bets. At Churchill Downs, odds are listed as a single number, such as 5. This translates to 5 to 1 odds, which means that you'd get a $5 payout for every $1 bet if said horse wins. Though there are payouts for second and third places, the winnings are impossible to calculate until the race has been run because they vary based on which three horses end up in the money and in what order. It's complicated. Don't worry about it.

Third, once you've picked a horse, decide how much you want to bet (there's a $2 minimum), and whether you want to bet on the horse to win, place (finish second), or show (finish third). Be aware that if you bet a horse to place, you get a payout if it wins or places, and if you bet a horse to show, you get a payout if it wins, places, or shows. The payout for a show bet on a winning horse isn't as much as the payout on a win bet, however.

Fourth, once you're certain you've picked the winner, head to the betting window. Approach the teller and place the bet. To make sure the teller gets all the info straight, give him your bet in the following manner: "Xth Race, X dollars to (win, place, show) on horse number X." (For example: "Fourth race, two dollars to win on number four.") Check your ticket before walking away from the window to make sure all the information is correct.

Finally, return to your seat and scream your lungs out in an effort to get your horse to cross the finish line first. If your horse does win (or place or show, depending on your wager) wait until the results are posted as final and then return to the betting window, where the teller will cash your ticket.

Once you've got the hang of the straight bet, you can venture into the world of exactas (pick in correct order the first and second place finishers), trifectas (pick in correct order the first, second, and third place finishers), pick threes (pick the winner of three designated races), and other exotic wagers, which someone at the race track will gladly explain to you if you just ask nicely. Good luck!

a winning Kentucky Derby ticket

© GREGORY DOWELL

Dark, a night racing event that tends to draw a younger crowd.

College Sports

Consistently drawing some of the largest crowds in college athletics, the **University of Louisville Cardinals** (502/852-5732, www. uoflsports.com) are Louisville's team. The men's basketball team, with a new home in the downtown KFC Yum! Center (S. 2nd St. and W. Main St.), is a crowd favorite, packing the 22,000-seat arena nearly every game. A perennial contender for the Big East Championship, as well as the National Championship, the Cards have made 35 appearances in the NCAA tournament, winning it all twice. The basketball rivalry with the cross-state Kentucky Wildcats is rabid, and was made even more so when the University of Louisville landed Rick Pitino as their head coach in 2001. For many Wildcat fans, this made Pitino a bigger traitor than Benedict Arnold himself, as Pitino had led the Cats for eight years in the 1990s, but for Louisville fans it was the coup of the century. No matter whom they're playing, however, expect exciting hoops and fans who live and die Cards basketball.

Behind men's basketball, U of L football is the passion of local fans, who religiously fill the 56,000 seats of Papa John's Cardinal Stadium (2800 S. Floyd St.) and go whole-hog in pregame tailgating. A stretch of highly successful seasons was crowned by a victory at the 2007 Orange Bowl, the Cards' first appearance in a BCS Bowl Game. Fortunes fell a bit after that when Coach Bobby Petrino departed, but with the hiring of Coach Charlie Strong for the 2010 season, the Cardinals are on the upswing and look to be a national contender once again.

Though overshadowed by men's basketball, the women's basketball program is also top-notch, playing for the national championship in 2009 but falling short to conference rival UConn despite having the top overall draft pick on the team. The women share KFC Yum! Center with the men's team.

Additionally, the Louisville baseball team has recently come into its own, appearing in the College World Series in 2007 and contending each year since for a top spot in the baseball rankings. The team plays at Jim Patterson Stadium (Central Ave. and 3rd St.).

Tickets may be purchased online at www.ticketmaster.com or www.stubhub.com, or at the U of L Ticket Offices (Belknap Campus,

MORE THAN A RIVALRY: THE NATION'S BIGGEST HIGH SCHOOL FOOTBALL GAME

On a Friday evening in late September, more than 35,000 fans pack Papa John's Cardinal Stadium to watch a football game, but not one played by the University of Louisville. Instead, these fans, wearing St. Xavier green-and-gold or Trinity green-and-white sweatshirts, face paint, and hats, have come to watch Louisville's two largest Catholic all-male high schools have it out on the gridiron. It's the nation's best high school football rivalry.

Year in and year out, one, if not both of these two teams, end up in the state championship game, but to many players and fans, the annual St. X-Trinity game is just as, if not more, important. Sure, the approximately 1,400 students from each high school attend, but so also do their parents, their neighbors, their friends, and their friends' friends. Alumni turn out with their families in tow, some coming all the way across the country to what has become an unofficial annual reunion. Tailgating reaches a fever pitch in the parking lot pre-game, though officials do ask that you keep it alcohol-free. Going far beyond a high school event, the St. X-Trinity game is a Louisville event, so no matter what your connection is, you'll want to join the crazed fans in seeing high school football like you've never seen it before.

Student Activities Center, 3rd Floor, Corner of Floyd St. and Brandeis St., 502/852-5151, or Papa John's Cardinal Stadium Gate 2, 9 A.M.–5 P.M. Mon.–Fri., and 9 A.M. game days). Tickets for baseball, field hockey, lacrosse, softball, swimming, and tennis are all free.

Professional Baseball

As the AAA-affiliate of the Cincinnati Reds, the **Louisville Bats** (502/212-2287, http://web.minorleaguebaseball.com) offer baseball fans a chance to see tomorrow's big-league stars in an intimate setting. The Bats play home games at **Louisville Slugger Field** (401 E. Main St.), a 13,000-seat stadium with views of downtown and the Ohio River. The stadium, which opened in 2000, preserves a part of historic Louisville in that it incorporates the Brinly-Hardy Warehouse, a train shed built in 1889, into its design. With tickets starting at $6, a Bats game at Slugger Field makes for a fun date, night out with friends, or family outing. Come early to get autographs, then enjoy the game, knowing that if the kids get restless, there are two in-stadium playgrounds, a carousel, a speed pitch activity, and the never-ending antics of mascot Buddy Bat.

Accommodations

Most visitors to Louisville will want to reserve a room in one of the downtown hotels or Old Louisville B&Bs. From either of these two areas, you can easily access the city's major sights and restaurants. Look for weekend deals downtown when business travelers have gone home, and mid-week specials at the B&Bs. Prices soar all over town at Derby time, and you'll also find higher prices in Old Louisville during the St. James Court Art Show.

Bardstown Road is also a great place to base yourself, but options are minimal. If you're looking for a retreat, the offerings in East Louisville are nice, but be aware that they're a bit removed from the action.

DOWNTOWN
$150-200

Though the current **Galt House** (140 N. 4th St., 502/589-5200, www.galthouse.com, $130–225) dates back to only 1971, the establishment's first incarnation played host to the likes of Jefferson Davis and Charles Dickens in the 1800s. Now the Galt House is the largest hotel in Kentucky and the only waterfront hotel in Louisville, its twin towers a distinctive part of the downtown skyline. For a view out onto the Ohio River, choose one of the 591 rooms in the Rivue Tower. Deluxe rooms are spacious but not special, while suites have the luxury of balconies, wet bars, and an extra half-bath. For an upgrade, choose the neighboring Suite Tower, which offers 600 premium rooms decked-out with all the amenities. The hotel is often used for large conventions, so you may want to inquire whom you will be sharing the hotel with when you reserve a room.

Over $200

One of Louisville's golden-era hotels, the four-star **Brown Hotel** (335 W. Broadway, 502/583-1234, www.brownhotel.com, $199–499) offers all the luxuries one expects from a hotel built in the high-rolling 1920s: a grand lobby fit for movie star entrances, marble flooring, mahogany furniture, and faultless service. If you can afford it, spring for one of the spacious suites, which honor the formal English Renaissance architecture of the hotel while remaining entirely comfortable. The deluxe rooms can be small and some are a bit threadbare, but worth the price if ambiance is your interest. Located in the theater district, the Brown is within easy walking distance of all downtown attractions.

If you're a *Great Gatsby* fan, then you can't pass on a night at the downtown **Seelbach Hotel** (500 4th St., 502/585-3200, www.

seelbachhilton.com, $229–280), the inspiration for the site of Tom and Daisy Buchanan's wedding in that famous book. Though now part of the Hilton family, the Seelbach shuns any efforts at conformity and clings to the old-world elegance that has attracted the likes of F. Scott Fitzgerald, Al Capone, and John F. Kennedy. All rooms feature Renaissance reproduction furniture including four-poster beds, Chippendale accents, and marble-clad bathrooms. But don't expect to spend too

much time in your well-appointed (though somewhat small) room; you'll be too busy having a bourbon in the Oak Room alcove where Capone played cards, sneaking a peek at the Grand Ballroom that inspired Fitzgerald, or admiring the medieval style of the Rathskellar, the only surviving Rookwood Pottery room in the world.

If you like modern, artsy, hip hotels, then check yourself into **◖ 21C Museum Hotel** (700 W. Main St., 502/217-6300,

FINDING ACCOMMODATIONS FOR THE DERBY

Locating a place to rest your bones during Derby week, and especially on Derby weekend, is not easy. It's also not cheap. But with persistence, a willingness to compromise, and a bit of money saved up, you can find something to fit your taste and budget.

If you're committed to doing the Derby up in high style, then you want to stay at one of downtown Louisville's classic hotels. In order to make this a reality you must do two things: 1) plan early, and 2) pay the big bucks. It's not uncommon for Derby regulars to book their next year's room when they arrive for the current year's Derby. For a choice of rooms, you'll want to begin planning by January, though you can pick through leftovers into early spring. Most of the downtown hotels only offer rooms as part of package deals and usually have a two- or three-night minimum. Expect to pay thousands of dollars for a weekend stay.

The B&Bs of Old Louisville also offer an excellent Derby experience, particularly if you like intimate spaces and the opportunity to get really personalized advice on how to best enjoy the Derby. They are also very well located, just 2.5 miles from Churchill Downs. Unfortunately, the biggest of Louisville's B&Bs have no more than eight rooms, and some have as few as two. This means that they book up quickly, often with repeat customers. Expect to pay rates much higher than average if you do manage to find a room.

For those less picky about the ambiance of their accommodations, but desirous of a location within city limits, Louisville's chain hotels

offer the best option. Come Derby Day you'll find that almost all of them are at capacity, but they don't fill as quickly as the local hotels, giving you a little more time to get your plans together. Be aware that you won't find any deals here, however. Prices generally start around $300 for a typical double room. Visit a hotel aggregator website such as www.hotels.com to sort through your options.

If $300 for the Holiday Inn sounds ludicrous to you, then start looking farther afield. Once you get outside of Louisville and the immediate surrounding communities, you'll find prices that more closely resemble regular rates. You'll have to drive further and won't have all the amenities of the city, but if your main goal is to make it to the Derby without breaking the bank, this is the way to go. Begin by checking for hotels in Southern Indiana (New Albany, Jeffersonville, Clarksville), La Grange, and Shepherdsville, where prices will range greatly but be more affordable overall. You can also consider making the Derby just part of a Kentucky vacation, opening up hotel possibilities in Bardstown (30 miles), Frankfort (50 miles), and Lexington (70 miles).

Finally, go local and look for apartments, condos, and homes available for lease during Derby week. More than a few Louisvillians move in with friends and family for the weekend, renting their digs to out-of-towners. For large groups, this can be an especially good deal. Check the vacation rental and sublet sections of www.craigslist.org for available properties.

www.21chotel.com, $240–485), the most innovative hotel in the state. Every one of the 90 rooms in this boutique hotel incorporates contemporary art into its design, but in no way is 21C too cool for school. Southern hospitality is the rule here, and the hotel doesn't just cover all the bases, it goes above and beyond with amenities like iPods, flat-screen HDTVs, wireless Internet, and silver mint julep cups in each room. Look for the red penguins adorning the roof of this hotel right in the heart of Museum Row.

OLD LOUISVILLE
$50-100

The three rooms at **Gallery House** (1386 S. 6th St., 502/635-2550, www.thegalleryhouse.com, $85–95) offer the most affordable stay in Old Louisville, though you should be aware that despite the home's High Victorian appearance, it was actually built in 1997 after a fire destroyed the previous property. The spirit of the house remains true to the neighborhood, and you'll enjoy the fact that all rooms have en suite bathrooms and modern systems. Plus it's hard to find owners better suited to the job: Gordon is an artist, meaning you'll find original artwork all over the house, and Leah is a chef, known for making some of the best wedding cakes in town, so you can bet that breakfast will be a treat.

$100-150

Slip back in time at ◖ **1888 Historic Rocking Horse Manor Bed and Breakfast** (1022 S. 3rd St., 502/583-0408, www.rockinghorse-bb.com, $105–195), a meticulously restored Richardsonian Romanesque mansion in the heart of Old Louisville. The attention to architectural detail—original stained glass, relaxing claw-foot soaking tubs, and splendidly carved fireplace mantels—is matched only by the attention afforded each guest by the innkeepers, who serve a delicious two-course breakfast each morning and provide snacks and drinks in the evening. Each of the six rooms is tastefully decorated in period style and has its own bathroom. For a splurge, go for the Victorian

Suite with its king-size canopy bed and hot tub. And don't worry, though this B&B's style is old-fashioned, the amenities are modern and include wireless Internet and cable TV.

Though the six rooms—all named for the innkeeper's family members—at **Aleksander House Bed and Breakfast** (1213 S. 1st St., 502/637-4985, www.aleksanderhouse.com, $115–195) have distinct feels, the overall vibe of this 1882 Victorian mansion is warm and inviting, like the French Impressionist paintings in the dining room. Among Aleksander House's more unique offerings is a suite that can sleep 4–6 people, making it perfect for a family or girlfriend getaway. Additionally, the gourmet breakfast menu offers equally delicious options for vegans, diabetics, and celiacs.

Austin's Inn Place (915 S. 1st St., 502/585-8855, www.austinsinnplace.com, $135–155) combines two three-story houses to offer guests a choice of eight rooms, each fitted with either a king or queen bed with top-of-the-line bedding. The expansive inn also offers plenty of communal space, including a library, bar, game room, and garden. Exposed red brick features throughout the inn, which was once the home of Kentucky governor Augustus Everett Willson. For those who rise before its time for the full breakfast, a spread of tea, coffee, juice, cereal, fruit, and pastries will help tide you over.

Step through the triple entry of the Richardsonian Romanesque **Bernheim Mansion** (1416 S. 3rd St., 502/235-3475, www.bernheimmansion.com, $119–225), and you'll immediately notice the abundance of exotic woods and intricate woodwork, as well as the curved stairwell lit by stained glass windows. This B&B is heavy on style and true to its roots as the home of distiller and philanthropist Bernhard Bernheim. If you're looking for luxury, choose between the Bernheim Suite and the Carriage House. The Bernheim Suite swells with old-world charm and includes a private library and office. The Carriage House impresses with its soaring 30-foot wood ceiling and exposed beams, combining contemporary architecture with antique decor. The less

COURTESY OF THE COLUMBINE BED & BREAKFAST

Columbine Bed and Breakfast

expensive of the five accommodation options have shared baths.

Thanks to its great columned portico and Greek Revival style, the ◖ **Columbine Bed and Breakfast** (1707 S. 3rd St., 502/635-5000, www.thecolumbine.com, $119–165) stands out in this neighborhood of Victorian homes. Guests also love its sunny porches, welcoming back garden, friendly innkeepers, and breakfasts with a raved-about homemade syrup. Built for a mahogany magnate in 1896, the house is filled with this sumptuous wood. It's also remarkably well decorated with the six large rooms classic and understated. If you fear frilliness, lace, and floral decor, then this is the B&B for you. The only negative is that bathrooms, though private, are often across the hall, but the plush bathrobes provided make this only a minor inconvenience.

One of the most magnificent homes on what was once known as Millionaire's Row, the 20,000-square-foot **Culbertson Mansion** (1432 S. 3rd St., 502/634-3100, www.culbertsonmansion.us, $109–179) boasts over 50 rooms, all decadently decorated, including the seven bedrooms available to guests. Built by Samuel Culbertson, president of Churchill Downs during the 1920s and '30s and the man behind the garland of roses awarded to the Derby winner, the mansion was home to many formal dinner parties and dances. Now whether you're entering through the marble mosaic door, savoring breakfast at the original dining table, having a complimentary drink with the hosts in the downstairs bar, or relaxing amidst the 100 varieties of roses in the formal courtyard, you'll feel like an honored guest. Splurge for the Knights of Kentucky Suite, replete with its own baby grand piano, and you'll feel like royalty.

$150-200

Built for the wealthy industrialist family for which it is named, the ◖ **DuPont Mansion** (1317 S. 4th St., 502/638-0045, www.dupontmansion.com, $129–239) is a conscientiously restored 1879 Italianate mansion with details that will make your jaw drop. While you eat breakfast under sparkling chandeliers, enjoy the murals covering the wall of the dining room. In the evening, take your snack of homemade goodies and wine in the formal gardens. And at night, luxuriate in the whirlpool tub found in each of the B&B's seven rooms. All of the rooms are elegant and decorated with period furniture and reproductions, but the two suites are particularly magnificent. If the DuPont Mansion is all booked up, check the availability at **Inn at the Park** (1332 S. 4th St., 502/638-0045, www.innatpark.com, $129–209), a sister property just across the street.

EAST LOUISVILLE
$100-150

Once you enter the **Inn at Woodhaven** (401 S. Hubbards Ln., 888/895-1011, www.innatwoodhaven.com, $105–225), a 19th-century Gothic Revival home painted a cheery yellow, you'll forget that the inn is located next to an apartment complex. Beautifully decorated with period furniture, the inn makes sure no detail is forgotten. Choose between four rooms in the main house, three rooms in the carriage house outback, or the octagonal Rose Cottage. The main house's Attic Room is bigger than most apartments; in fact, the bathroom with its spa tub and steam shower for two is bigger than most hotel rooms. Enjoy the three-course gourmet breakfast in the dining room or in the comfort of your own room.

While most B&Bs are from the Victorian era, **Tucker House Bed and Breakfast** (2406 Tucker Station Rd., 502/297-8007, www.tuckerhouse1840.com, $105–125) transports you to the era of antebellum country living, with its four bed chambers, dining areas, and living areas all decorated true to the 1840s. Located a bit outside of town, the brick Federal-style Tucker House is a great place to stay if you're looking for a true getaway, especially if you love peace and quiet and the great outdoors. Bring your hiking shoes to explore the five acres of woods and the spring-fed lake. As much as you'll love the period decor, you'll also enjoy the modern pool, decks, and amenities.

BARDSTOWN ROAD
$100-150

Secure residence in one of Louisville's favorite neighborhoods, The Highlands, with a room at **The Roost Inn** (1325 Bardstown Rd., 502/451-0121, www.bbonline.com/ky/alley, $105–145). Innkeeper Annette Saco also owns the rustic Italian restaurant Le Gallo Rosso, which is located in the same building and will tempt you with the smells of lasagna until you make dinner reservations. All four suites have their own entrances, bathrooms, and kitchens. Breakfast is continental-style but brought to your room. Weekly and monthly rates make The Roost Inn a good long-term option.

Food

Louisville has a remarkable food scene that easily blows away the competition from any city of similar size and holds its own quite well against cities of bigger size and stature. Many of Louisville's restaurants have received national recognition, and even if you're used to the NYC dining scene, you'll find something to impress you here in Louisville. Whether you're on a college student budget or putting the bill on your boss's tab, whether you're in the mood for Southern-style home cooking or out-of-this-world ethnic fare, one of Louisville's local restaurants will gladly see you satisfied. Reservations are never a bad idea at any of Louisville's restaurants.

If you don't see what you're looking for in the listings here, visit www.louisvillehotbytes.com, a food guide site created by Robin Garr, the former *Courier-Journal* food critic and a man who knows good food. The site offers extensive reviews, which you can sort by location, price, or food type, and also hosts a forum where you can get advice from locals.

LOUISVILLE'S CATHOLIC LEGACY

With over 100 parishes in the Archdiocese of Louisville and over 20,000 students attending Catholic schools in Louisville, the Catholic Church holds strong influence in the city, not surprising if you consider that many Louisvillians come from Catholic German, Irish, and French stock. Though certainly not the only faith in town – both the Southern Baptists and Presbyterians have important seminaries in the city with congregations to match, Southeast Christian Church is one of the nation's largest megachurches, and residents of nearly every faith can find a church home in Louisville – the Catholic Church has a way of injecting itself into the city's cultural life. Two of the more popular ways, which cross faith boundaries to bring people of varied beliefs together, are Friday fish fries and parish picnics.

On Fridays in Lent, nearly every Catholic parish puts on a fish fry, where for a low price anyone is welcome to feast on a plate of fish and Southern sides (think mac 'n' cheese, green beans, and the like). Stop in at the Catholic church nearest you to find out the schedule; if they're not hosting one, they'll know where the nearest one is.

In summer, there's not a single weekend that's church picnic free. These aren't low-key affairs, but rather big events where the beer and brats flow freely, carnival rides keep the kids happy, and booths offer the chance for you to win a cake, a tin of popcorn, or an enormous stuffed animal. One of the most popular picnics is August's St. Joseph Orphan's Picnic (2823 Frankfort Ave.), which brings volunteers from parishes all over the city together to man over 60 booths, with all proceeds benefiting the St. Joseph Children's Home. For a schedule of picnics, visit the Archdiocese of Louisville's website (www.archlou.org).

DOWNTOWN
Quick Eats

Though their main clientele is downtown workers on short lunch breaks, **Main Eatery** (643 W. Main St., 502/589-7200, 11 A.M.–2 P.M. Mon.–Fri., $3.95–6.95) is a great place to grab a bite between museum visits, at least on weekdays. Their soups and sandwiches are always fresh and filling, and though the line can be long, it moves fast. Try the chicken salad and the tomato bisque.

For a quick lunch stop between museum visits that will please the entire family, pop in to **Luigi's Pizzeria and Pasta** (712 W. Main St., 502/589-0005, www.luigispizzeria.com, 7 A.M.–5 P.M. Mon.–Fri., 11 A.M.–3 P.M. Sat., $2.99–6.95). Scope out the ready-made pizzas (by the pie or the slice), pastas, subs, and specialty sandwiches, then place your order at the counter. If you're just passing by on the sidewalk, be prepared for the aroma to draw you in.

Cafés

If you're in the mood for a good sandwich—hearty bread, crisp vegetables, savory meats, and tasty dressings—but want a little atmosphere on the side, grab a seat at **The Café** (712 Brent St., 502/589-9191, www.thecafe-togo.com, 8 A.M.–4 P.M. daily, $4.95–8.95), where the tables are decked in white linens and spruced up with fresh flowers. The sandwiches (of which there are nearly 20) are so big you'll probably end up taking half home, and each comes with a choice of a fresh side. Try the bean salad. A wide variety of soups and salads round out the lunch menu, while the breakfast menu offers a selection of baked goods as well as filling entrées like biscuits and gravy, twice-baked French toast, and Southern grits scramble.

Casual American

With six on-tap microbrews ranging from pale ale to porter as well as seasonal specialties, **Bluegrass Brewing Company** (660 S. 4th St., 502/568-2224, www.bbcbrew.com, 11 A.M.–10 P.M. Mon.–Thurs., 11 A.M.–11 P.M. Fri.–Sat., $7.99–11.99) is a great place to taste some local award-winning beer. Accompany your drink with a plate from the fine menu of pub grub, which features salads, sandwiches, and build-your-own pizza and burgers, including a unique spinach and walnut twist on the veggie burger. Atmosphere is lively and casual, as you'd expect from a brewpub.

If you're planning to catch a Louisville Bats baseball game, come early and have dinner at **Browning's Brewery and Restaurant** (401 E. Main St., 502/515-0174, www.browningsbrewery.com, 11 A.M.–10 P.M. Mon.–Fri., 4–10 P.M. Sat., 3–9 P.M. Sun., $8–16), located at Slugger Field. Typical bar and grill offerings—burgers, sandwiches, pasta, steak, and fish—will satisfy your hunger. The real reason to come to Browning's is for the beer, which is handcrafted on-site. Order one of the many appetizers and enjoy a few quality beers before you go into the game and overpay for cheap beer.

Southern
White Oak (620 E. Market St., 502/583-4177, www.thewhiteoakrestaurant.com, 11 A.M.–2 P.M. Mon.–Fri., 5–10 P.M. Tues.–Sat., $11–20) takes almost exclusively local food and creates delicious plates of comfort food. Down-home favorites like red wine beef stew, "Louisville" fried chicken, and cornmeal-dusted catfish are even better than you remember thanks to the chef's nuanced touch. At lunchtime, the menu ($8–12) features a few sandwiches, including pimento cheese and Benedictine with bacon, along with smaller portions of favorite dinner entrées. Live music complements your meal on Wednesday, Friday, and Saturday, and the courtyard is heated for year-round comfort. With unique art decking the wall, the ambiance is akin to eating in a very cool, but comfy, art gallery.

Contemporary American
732 Social (732 E. Market St., 502/583-6882, www.732social.com, 5 P.M.–midnight Mon.–Thurs., 5 P.M.–1 A.M. Fri.–Sat., $14–26) is pushing boundaries by getting back to our roots. Located in the Green Building, a LEED-certified mixed-use building, 732 Social serves farm-to-table food and organic wines. Though focusing on fresh and sustainable foods, the menu is varied and might offer everything from tagine of Moroccan vegetables to pork and cabbage. Choose from small plates, large plates, or plates for the whole table, as well as cheese and meat plates. Fresh and modern, the restaurant keeps things natural with full-length windows, high ceilings, and tables made from reclaimed wood from a tobacco barn. 732 Social lives up to its name and is often crowded and can get very loud.

Breakfast
Momma knew what she was talking about when she said breakfast was the most important meal of the day, so visit **Toast on Market** (736 E. Market St., 502/569-4099, www.toastonmarket.com, 7 A.M.–2 P.M. Tues.–Fri., 7 A.M.–3 P.M. Sat.–Sun., $4.75–11.50) to get your day started right. The King French Toast, a tribute to Elvis with its peanut butter and bananas, will get you singing, while Cliffie's Plate, involving eggs, meat, hashbrown casserole, and pancakes, makes eating the rest of the day optional. A selection of sandwiches and salads is available for those who refuse to listen to their mothers. Oversized artwork and exposed brick give Toast on Market a fun, laid-back feel.

Hotel Restaurants
As innovative as the hotel in which it is located, 21C's **Proof on Main** (702 W. Main St., 502/217-6360, 11 A.M.–2 P.M. Mon.–Fri. lunch, 5:30–11 P.M. Sun.–Thurs., 5 P.M.–midnight Fri.–Sat., $15–29) combines Tuscan influence and Southern flavors to create an eccentric menu highlighted by heaps of local and artisanal ingredients. On the daily specials menu you might find Kentucky bison tenderloin or fried local rabbit. The cured meat platter makes a nice starter, and for dessert try the house-made gelato and sorbet. The bold artwork for which the hotel is known continues in Proof, and the design is modern yet inviting.

On the 25th floor of the Galt House, you'll find **Rivue** (140 N. 4th St., 502/568-4239, www.rivue.com, 5:30–10:30 P.M. Tues.–Sat., 10 A.M.–3 P.M. Sun., $21–36) and its two revolving dining rooms, which offer unbeatable views of downtown and the river. The red, white, and black Art Deco design works for this powerhouse restaurant, where the menu leans heavily to steak, seafood, and pasta—dishes that while expected are also exceptionally well done.

Extravagance is the name of the game at the Seelbach's **Oak Room** (500 4th St., 502/807-3463, www.theoakroomlouisville.com, 5:30–10:30 P.M. Tues.–Sat., 10 A.M.–2 P.M. Sun., $24–40), which boasts the city's largest wine cellar, a bourbon menu with over 40 choices, a lavish formal dining room, and a five-diamond AAA rating. On the menu, you'll find such riches as foie gras, Maine lobster, and duck, all prepared traditionally. If you're looking to seal the deal—in business or romance—consider the Oak Room.

Though the Brown's **English Grill** is excellent for formal dining, for a casual meal bypass it for **J. Graham's Café** (335 W. Broadway, 502/583-1234, www.brownhotel.com, 7 A.M.–2 P.M. daily, $10–14). You don't need to bother with a menu, just ask for the Hot Brown, a Louisville signature dish consisting of an open-faced roasted turkey sandwich smothered in Mornay sauce, parmesan cheese, tomato, and bacon and baked into a gooey delicious mess. It was invented at the Brown in 1926. Finish your meal with a slice of original Derby Pie, and you'll have had a truly local lunch.

Italian

Fitting in just fine with the art galleries around it, **Primo** (445 E. Market St., 502/583-1808, www.primorestaurant.net, 11:30 A.M.–2:30 P.M. and 5:30–10 P.M. Mon.–Thurs., 11:30 A.M.–2:30 P.M. and 5:30–11 P.M. Fri., 5:30–11 P.M. Sat., $13–29) is an innovative and chic restaurant, serving up the best traditional and contemporary food coming out of Italy. The dinner menu changes weekly, but always remains focused with just a few selections in each category: antipasto, salads, pizzas, pasta, seafood, and steak and chops. The individual-size pizzas are thin and crispy and range from the simple but classic Margherita to a pie topped with shrimp, spinach, and garlic

butter. Pastas choices might include tagliatelle with veal meatballs or linguine with littleneck clams, arugula, and red chile. A lunch menu ($9–13) is available. The contemporary-style restaurant has a strong urban vibe with window-side booths providing street views.

Latin American

If you like your Latin food authentic, then you'll want to grab a table at █ **Mayan Café** (813 E. Market St., 502/566-0651, www.themayancafe.com, 11 A.M.–2:30 P.M. and 5–10 P.M. Mon.–Fri., 5–10:30 P.M. Sat., $10–19), where smoky notes of chile play a central role in the flavor of each dish. With heavy Mayan influence, the food at this chic but casual hotspot is nothing like what you get at a typical Mexican restaurant. Check out the chef's specials; his salbutes (topped corn tortillas) have garnered acclaim since his days driving a taco truck, and the catch of the day is always as fresh as the produce Chef Ucan buys at the local farmers market. Regardless of how you think you feel about lima beans, order them as your side. Trust me on this one. The very small restaurant feels airy thanks to its sky-blue walls and clean lines, and sidewalk seating is available when the weather's nice.

Dessert

Only the finest natural ingredients go into the sweet treats baked daily at **Cake Flour** (909 E. Market St., 502/719-0172, www.cakeflouronmarket.com, 7 A.M.–2 P.M. Mon., 7 A.M.–6 P.M. Tues.–Fri., 8 A.M.–2 P.M. Sat.–Sun.). White chocolate cheesecake, banana truffle cupcakes, and lemon tarts are just some of the tempting goodies on offer.

Stop in **Muth's Candies** (630 E. Market St., 502/585-2952, www.muthscandy.com, 8:30 A.M.–4 P.M. Tues.–Fri., 10 A.M.–4 P.M. Sat.), Louisville's confectionary since 1921, to stock up on candy made the old-fashioned way. An assortment of bourbon candies, caramels, turtles, and modjeskas—a caramel and marshmallow treat created locally and named in honor of a famous Polish actress—will keep you happy for at least a day.

OLD LOUISVILLE
Cafés

You'll feel like you stepped inside from a French boulevard rather than the streets of Old Louisville when you enter **Ermin's Bakery and Café** (1201 S. 1st St., 502/635-6960, www.erminsbakery.com, 7 A.M.–7 P.M. Mon.–Fri., 8 A.M.–5 P.M. Sat., 9 A.M.–3 P.M. Sun. $3.95–6.95), especially when your eyes come to rest on the pastry displays. Artisan homemade breads are still cooked in imported European ovens, and the pastries are lovingly made each day. Just try choosing between the cinnamon roll and apple strudel for breakfast or the petit four and sin bar (a rich combination of chocolate and peanut butter) for dessert. Whatever you end up with, your sweet tooth will be satisfied. If you just have to eat lunch before indulging in dessert, well you're in luck, as Ermin's knows how to make a sandwich. Pair your half-sandwich of choice with the house tomato basil soup for a filling meal.

Casual American

Popular with U of L students, the **Granville Inn** (1601 S. Third St., 502/635-6475, 11 A.M.–1 A.M. daily, $3.95–7.95) is a constant competitor for the title of Best Burger. The signature burger is a half-pound of hand-formed beef charbroiled to order and topped with lettuce, tomato, onion, and cheese and served with a heaping side of fries. The pizzas, which come in three sizes, are also popular. Top your own or choose one of the specialty pizzas, like The Meat Man Cometh. The bar serves up stiff cocktails as well as cheap pints of craft draft beer, favored by the college crowd. The atmosphere is that of a local joint—a bit dark, with TVs, electronic dartboards, and a pool table—but the staff is friendly and if you come in a time or two you can be pretty sure that they'll remember your name.

Contemporary American

If you consider yourself a gourmand, make a reservation at **610 Magnolia** (610 W. Magnolia Ave., 502/636-0783, www.610magnolia.com, Thurs.–Sat., dinner only, reservations required) and prepare to be wowed. Widely considered to be one of the best restaurants in the region, the elegant but minimalist 610 Magnolia offers three prix-fixe menus that change every night, but always center around in-season, local, organic ingredients. Choose between three ($45), four ($55), or six courses ($65), as well as vegetarian versions of each menu. What exactly will end up on your plate is a surprise, but Chef Edward Lee consistently turns out sophisticated American food—think venison, boar, scallops, bass, duck, and quail—enhanced with global flavors. A wine pairing is available for $45. The atmosphere of this house restaurant is understated, creating an elegant and intimate setting for a special occasion dinner.

SOUTH LOUISVILLE
Diners

If you like to talk horse racing while you eat, stop in at **Wagner's Pharmacy** (3113 S. 4th St., 502/375-3800, www.wagnerspharmacy.com, 8 A.M.–2:30 P.M. Mon.–Fri., 8 A.M.–noon Sat. as well as Sun. during racing meets, $2.75–7.50), just across the street from Churchill Downs. Since 1922, Wagner's has been the gathering place for those in the horse industry, and inside the simple white building decorated with images of Derby winners you're likely to share the lunch counter with jockeys, trainers, and owners. The diner-style menu is simple: lunch is a choice between a long list of sandwiches and the daily special (roast beef on Wednesday, fried fish on Friday), while breakfast options include a selection of omelettes; à la carte pancakes; and platters with your choice of ham, sausage, or bacon with eggs, biscuits, and potatoes.

Asian

Don't let its strip mall location mislead you. It might not look like much, but **Vietnam Kitchen** (5339 Mitscher Ave., 502/363-5154, 11 A.M.–10 P.M. Sun.–Tues. and Thurs., 11 A.M.–11 P.M. Fri.–Sat., $6.50–11.95) is where Louisville's many Vietnamese immigrants come to be transported back home. From the staple pho (rice-noodle soup traditionally served with beef) to meat, seafood, and vegetarian stir-fry, curry, and clay-pot dishes, the taste will take you to the other side of the world. Vegetarian options abound, and the spice level of each dish can be adjusted, but you'll have to be pretty convincing to get the friendly staff to serve it to you "Vietnam Spicy," as that level of heat is enough to knock most people out of their seats.

FRANKFORT AVENUE
Contemporary American

With over 80 different offerings that can be enjoyed in two-ounce tastes, six-ounce glasses, or by the bottle, wine is the star at the **L&N Wine Bar & Bistro** (1765 Mellwood Ave., 502/897-0070, www.landnwinebarandbistro. com, 5–11 P.M. Mon.–Sat., $13–28). You're more than welcome to savor the varietals at the bar in this warm establishment with brick interiors, glowing fireplaces, and plush chairs, or you can have a seat and pair your wine with some food. Perhaps you just want to go with appetizers—a cheese plate or lamb pops—or maybe dessert—the Belgian chocolate fondue is date-perfect—or you can make it a meal with the well-regarded steak frites or vegetable Wellington.

Barbecue

The **Frankfort Avenue Beer Depot** (3204 Frankfort Ave., 502/895-3223, 10 A.M.–2 A.M. Mon.–Sat., $4–12), is a super casual joint, basically a dive, that serves amazing brisket, ribs, chicken, and pulled pork, smoked right in the front parking lot, along with fantastic coleslaw, potato salad, baked beans, macaroni and cheese, and spicy fries. As the name suggests, there's plenty of beer on offer, and many people come by just to have a drink and play the mini golf course out back or a round of cornhole.

Asian

At **◖ Basa** (2244 Frankfort Ave., 502/896-1016, www.basarestaurant.com, 5–10 P.M.

Mon.–Thurs., 5–11 P.M. Fri.–Sat., $15–29), a 2008 James Beard Best New Restaurant semi-finalist, local ingredients are transformed into tantalizing modern Vietnamese cuisine. The menu is small and focused, with many of the appetizers and entrées featuring seafood—prawns, tuna, oysters, mussels, and the like. One of the most raved about entrées, however, is the Shaking Beef, cubed filet mignon cooked with garlic, watercress, cherry tomatoes, and red onions in a very hot wok. Expect elegant presentation and fine service at one of Louisville's hottest restaurants.

Not your typical sushi bar, **Maido** (1758 Frankfort Ave., 502/894-8775, www.maidosakebar.com, 4–10 P.M. Mon.–Thurs., 4–11 P.M. Fri.–Sat., small plates $4–8) is an izakaya-style restaurant—a combination pub, sake bar, and eatery popular in the Osaka area of Japan. The shotgun house cum funky Japanese restaurant with a lively patio is a place you want to go with friends so that you can order a large selection of the small plates—ranging from kimchi pork to avocado tempura to *kushikatsu* (skewered meat or vegetables coated in panko and deep fried)—as well as a few servings of sushi (the citrus heat roll has locals talking). If you're a sake fan, Maido has the best selection in town, and their list of microbrews is pretty impressive too.

European

Fashioning itself as a traditional Irish pub, the **Irish Rover** (2319 Frankfort Ave., 502/899-3544. www.theirishroverky.com, 11:30 A.M.–11 P.M. Mon.–Thurs., 11:30 A.M.–midnight Fri.–Sat., $5.95–14.95) is where the large percentage of Louisvillians who claim Irish heritage come for a taste of the old country. The menu features such hearty standards as fish and chips, bangers and mash, smoked salmon and potato gratin, and cottage pie—a bread bowl filled with steaming Guinness beef stew and topped with mashed potatoes and cheese. You won't go home hungry. And if you're thirsty, don't worry. The bar serves up a healthy

© THERESA DOWELL BLACKINTON

the Irish Rover, offering hearty pub fare

supply of whiskey as well as Guinness imported straight from Dublin.

Mediterranean

If you're looking to impress, head to **Varanese** (2106 Frankfort Ave., 502/899-9904, www.varanese.com, 5–11 P.M. Sun.–Thurs., 5 P.M.–midnight Fri.–Sat., $16–22), where the contemporary Mediterranean food, the nightly live jazz, the spot-on service, and the luscious atmosphere created by a stone waterwall and floor-to-ceiling windows come together to make Varanese one of Louisville's favorite destinations for a night out. The menu is creative, with occasional Southern touches gracing the Mediterranean dishes, and the prices are more than fair for the experience.

Latin American

Neighborhood anchor **El Mundo** (2345 Frankfort Ave., 502/899-9930, www.502elmundo.com, 11:30 A.M.–10 P.M. Tues.–Sun., $7.25–13.95) serves up Mexican food with a twist. In addition to burritos, enchiladas, and other favorites, the menu includes such unusual items as oyster crispy tacos. The fish tacos with fried cod and the grilled fajitas of the day are always a good choice, and the margaritas and sangria are top-notch. The two-story brick facade restaurant offers counter service downstairs and waiter service upstairs and on the patio. It's a tight space, so expect to get friendly with your neighbors and to wait if you come at peak hours.

Dessert

What is life without dessert? **Sweet Surrender Dessert Café** (1804 Frankfort Ave., 502/899-2008, www.sweetsurrenderdessertcafe.com, 10 A.M.–10 P.M. Tues.–Thurs., 10 A.M.–11 P.M. Fri.–Sat., $2–6) certainly makes you wonder that, with its sinful selection of cakes, tortes, pies, cupcakes, cookies, and dessert bars. Selection varies, which means that if your favorite is unavailable, you'll just have to come up with a new favorite. It's not hard to do. And unlike all the bakeries that close before the sun even sets, Sweet Surrender stays open well past dark so you can satisfy your late-night sweet tooth.

EAST LOUISVILLE
American

Located at Harrods Creek on the Ohio River, **Captain's Quarters** (5700 Captain's Quarter Rd., 502/228-1651, www.cqriverside.com, 11:30 A.M.–10 P.M. Mon.–Thurs., 11:30 A.M.–11 P.M. Fri.–Sat., 10:30 A.M.–10 P.M. Sun., $7.95–17.95) is Louisville's go-to restaurant for casual riverside dining. Though the dining room is bright and spacious with windows providing water views, it's the multi-level deck overlooking the river that attracts people to Captain's Quarter. As you might expect, the menu is heavy on seafood, offering fried cod, pan-seared salmon, seafood tortellini, and more, in addition to sandwiches, pizzas, and chicken and beef entrées. The fried banana peppers are a favorite of the happy hour crowd. Captain's Quarters offers tie-ups for hungry or thirsty boaters.

Asian

You can stick to your favorite Americanized Chinese dish at **Red Pepper Chinese Cuisine** (2901 Brownsboro Rd., 502/891-8868 www.redpepperchinesecuisine.com, 11 A.M.–9:30 P.M. Sun.–Thurs., 11 A.M.–10:30 P.M. Fri.–Sat., $6.95–12.95), but for a real taste of Szechwan-style cooking ask for the authentic Chinese menu. Don't worry, it's in English, though some of the translations are a bit comical (like A15, Unique Chicken Smell). Go ahead and skip the intestines (unless that's your thing), but dare to try all the other offerings. The hot pot dishes are both tasty and fun, served in a small wok over a flame. If you can't handle the heat that Szechwan cooking is known for, they'll happily tone done any dish. Since opening in late 2007, Red Pepper Chinese has been packing the house and is now the go-to place for many Chinese food lovers.

Breakfast

Regardless of whether you come for breakfast, brunch, or lunch, you want to order breakfast at **Wild Eggs** (3985 Dutchmans Ln., 502/893-8005, www.crackinwildeggs.com, 6:30 A.M.–2:30 P.M. Mon.–Fri., 7 A.M.–3 P.M. Sat.–Sun., $4.50–11.95). It's not that the soups and sandwiches aren't good; it's that the breakfast is great. As you'd expect from the name, you can get eggs any way you want them—served Tex-Mex or Benedict style, in omelettes or burritos, in scrambles and skillets. If the thought of eggs isn't making you go wild, then choose from a variety of other breakfast favorites like stuffed French toast or four different styles of pancakes and waffles. With its intimate arrangement, bright yellow and soft blue decor, and modern art, you feel a bit like you're having breakfast at a really cool relative's house.

Caribbean

Since most of us can't legally travel to Cuba, the best we can do to get a taste of the bright flavors of that forbidden Caribbean island is have a meal at **C Havana Rumba** (4115 Oechsli Ave., 502/897-1959, www.myhavanarumba.com, 11 A.M.–9:30 P.M. Mon.–Thurs., 11 A.M.–10 P.M. Fri., noon–10 P.M. Sat., noon–8:30 P.M. Sun., $7.50–15.99), where the Cuban-born chef-owner dishes up family recipes in a warm, festive atmosphere. The appetizer *papas rellenos* (mashed potato balls filled with seasoned ground beef) easily make a meal, and the namesake sandwich takes a standard Cubano (roasted pork, ham, Swiss cheese, pickles, and mustard hot-pressed on Cuban bread) and adds Serrano ham and Spanish chorizo. Mmm. The extensive menu also offers chicken, pork, beef, vegetable, and seafood entrées. While waiting for a seat, enjoy a drink at the always-buzzing mojito bar.

BARDSTOWN ROAD AREA

Known as Restaurant Row, Bardstown Road in the Highlands has a restaurant for every taste and every budget. If you're not sure what you're in the mood for, just start walking, checking out the menus at the many close-together restaurants. You're certain to find one that calls your name.

Contemporary American

Exuberant is the best way to describe **Café Lou Lou** (2216 Dundee Rd., 502/893-7776, www. cafeloulou.com, 11 A.M.–10 P.M. Sun.–Thurs., 11 A.M.–11 P.M. Fri.–Sat., $9.25–11.95), a fun and funky favorite with bold decor (think vivid colors and eye-catching art), spunky servers, and creative food. Though at first glance, the menu seems strongly Italian/Mediterranean thanks to its wide selection of pastas and pizzas, a closer look will reveal the chef's Louisiana and Louisville connections. Pasta jambalaya, muffaletta sandwiches, and Hot Brown pizzas share space with Italian meatball calzones, spinach and tomato crispy lavash, and bleu cheese polenta. In addition to doing its part to keep Louisville weird, Café Lou Lou is also helping to make Louisville delicious.

A neighborhood tavern from the 1930s to the 1970s, **Jack Fry's** (1007 Bardstown Rd., 502/452-9244, www.jackfrys.com, lunch 11 A.M.–2:30 P.M. Mon.–Fri., dinner 5:30–11 P.M. Mon.–Thurs., 5:30 P.M.–midnight Fri.–Sat., 5:30–10 P.M. Sun., $16–34) still retains a comfy, casual feel though the quality of food and the prices at this American bistro are decidedly upscale. The shrimp and grits appetizer is a signature dish and the potato gratin is a standout whether you're vegetarian or not. For those on a budget that doesn't accommodate lobster campanelle or the venison strip loin, the famous Jack's Burger is under $10, and the lunch menu is in the thrifty $9–12 range.

Long before it was the cool thing to do, **Lilly's** (1147 Bardstown Rd., 502/451-0477, www.lillyslapeche.com, 11 A.M.–3 P.M. and 5–10 P.M. Tues.–Sat., $12–28) established an award-winning menu based almost exclusively on locally sourced food. In fact, they even have their own organic garden, so the vegetables in your beet and carrot salad or the zucchini in your veal scallopine may have been picked just an hour before ending up on your plate. The menu changes seasonally, and though the food is local, this isn't down-home cooking, but rather refined dishes influenced by international flavors. Sleek and sophisticated in both look and taste, Lilly's is a landmark Louisville restaurant.

Asian

The cooking as well as the decor is bright and crisp at **Asiatique** (1767 Bardstown Rd., 502/451-2749, www.asiatiquerestaurant.com, 5–10:30 P.M. Mon.–Thurs., 5–11 P.M. Fri., noon–3 P.M. and 5–11 P.M. Sat., noon–3 P.M. Sun. $16–26), an upscale Pacific Rim restaurant with a global view. Malaysian-born Chef Looi, who has been a guest chef at the James Beard Foundation four times, turns out well-executed and mouthwatering cuisine, which changes seasonally, though favorites like the wok-seared salmon usually aren't off the menu for long. Five-course tasting menus (meat, seafood, and vegetarian) are also offered nightly.

Dragon King's Daughter (1126 Bardstown Rd., 602/632-2444, www.dragonkingsdaughter.com, 3 P.M.–midnight Mon.–Wed., noon–midnight Thurs.–Sat., noon–10 P.M. Sun., $8–12) gets creative with sushi, tempura, teriyaki, and other traditional Japanese dishes. For example, you can order a sashimi pizza, made with long strips of red tuna, white tuna, and salmon laid on top of mixed greens and placed on a piece of flatbread dressed with Japanese mayo. It sounds odd but it's delicious. Or maybe you're craving tacos. You could then order a shrimp tempura, Asian barbecue beef, or sautéed octopus taco. Regular sushi rolls are available along with a selection of snacks—sashimi salad, wasabi salsa, or ginger-garlic chicken wings. Located in a combined storefront with vividly painted walls hung with artwork for sale, high ceilings, hardwood floors, and an open layout, the restaurant is a casual place that can get a bit noisy. The happy hour menu (3–5 P.M. and 10 P.M.–midnight daily) is hard to beat.

Barbecue

In the tradition of good barbecue restaurants, **Mark's Feed Store** (1514 Bardstown Rd., 502/458-1570, www.marksfeedstore.com, 11 A.M.–10 P.M. Sun.–Thurs., 11 A.M.–11 P.M.

Fri.–Sat., $6.29–11.99) keeps things simple. Choose between pork, beef, or chicken sandwiches or platters, or a rack of fall-off-the-bone ribs. Everything's hickory smoked, and in Kentucky barbecue style doused with thick and slightly spicy sauce. Sides are what you'd expect: spicy fries, coleslaw, baked apples, baked beans, and the like. On Mondays after 4 P.M., you'll get a free dessert with your entrée.

Indian

Find all your northern Indian favorites—kormas, curries, thalis, tandooris, samosas, naans, lassis, and the like—at **Kashmir Indian Restaurant** (1285 Bardstown Rd., 502/473-8765, www.kashmirlouisville.com, 11:30 A.M.–3 P.M. and 5–10 P.M. Sun.–Thurs., noon–10:30 P.M. Fri.–Sat., $7.95–14.99). The weekend lunch buffet (noon–3 P.M. Sat.–Tues., $7.99), with over a dozen selections, is a crowd pleaser, and the regular lunch menu, with many dishes under $6, makes an Indian lunch a bargain option.

International

◖ **Ramsi's Café on the World** (1293 Bardstown Rd., 502/451-0700, www.ramsiscafe.com, 11 A.M.–1 A.M. Mon.–Thurs., 11 A.M.–2 A.M. Fri.–Sat., 10 A.M.–11 P.M. Sun., $8.95–17.95) isn't kidding about the world part. Though Ramsi and his family hail from Lebanon, their restaurant serves up dishes from all over the map, and they aren't afraid to mix and match the best of what the world has to offer. The East Meets South Fajitas, for instance, take traditional fajita ingredients and wrap them in Indian paratha bread, while the ribs are served with a Caribbean-style mango sauce. Vegetarians are generously catered for. Expect large portions, an eclectic and friendly staff, and on weekend evenings, a possible wait thanks to all the loyal local patrons. But don't worry, they'll come next door and get you from Carmichael's Bookstore when your table in one of the vibrantly decorated rooms complete with mismatched furniture or on the large, lovely patio becomes available.

Latin American

Named for the trendy neighborhood in Buenos Aires, **Palermo Viejo** (1359 Bardstown Rd., 502/456-6461, 5–11 P.M. Mon.–Sat., $12–17) serves up the mean steaks for which Argentina is known and doesn't forget the chimichurri on the side. True meat lovers can indulge in the *parrillada*, a mixed grill of chorizo, short ribs, tenderloin, and sweetbreads. Order a side of the parsley and garlic fries to complete your meal. In a nod to other popular Argentinean cuisine, the menu also offers empanadas and a selection of pasta. In summer, when you can sit outdoors and people-watch, the small restaurant gains a few seats. Inside the narrow dining room, where exposed brick is complemented by unfinished oak, you can choose to sit up front with a view of the street or in the back with a view of the open kitchen.

Garnering national recognition for its Nuevo Latino cuisine, ◖ **Seviche** (1538 Bardstown Rd., 502/473-8560, www.sevicherestaurant.com, 5–10 P.M. Mon.–Thurs., 5–11 P.M. Fri.–Sat., 5–9 P.M. Sun., $13–29) has introduced local palates to the fresh, bright tastes of authentic food from south of the border. As the name suggests, seafood plays a prominent role on the menu, both as entrées and in the namesake seviches, of which there are at least eight different varieties available each day. A tasting menu of seviches is available for the true aficionado of this zesty Latin American specialty involving seafood "cooked" by its citrus marinade. Dressed-up empanadas, such as one with goat cheese and wild mushrooms, find a place on the appetizer list, while a few steak dishes and a chicken and a vegetable option round out the entrées. In a more modern building than most Bardstown Road restaurants, Seviche has a fresh, bright feel, with large windows that let in a lot of light as well as allow for good people watching. A 2010 expansion doubled the size of the restaurant.

Mediterranean

Take it from a girl who spent a year in Greece eating gyros every day, **Zaytun** (2286 Bardstown Rd., 502/365-1788,

11:30 A.M.–10 P.M. Tues.–Thurs., 11:30 A.M.–11 P.M. Fri.–Sat., noon–9 P.M.Sun., $7.95–$11.95) has the best gyros in town. The pita isn't traditional, more of a flatbread instead, but it's delicious, and the meat (choose between chicken or a mix of lamb and beef) is seasoned, cooked, and cut just right. Go traditional at this small, casual eatery and top your gyro only with tomato, onion, and tzatziki, or add extra touches like lettuce, olives, and feta cheese. If you're wondering about the slightly out-of-place fried fish on the menu, it comes from **Sharom's** (5637 Outer Loop, 502/968-8363, www.sharoms.com, 11 A.M.–9 P.M. Mon.–Thurs., 11 A.M.–10 P.M. Fri., noon–9 P.M. Sat., noon–10 P.M. Sun., $8.50–11.50), the excellent South Louisville fish restaurant owned by proprietor Remi Pouranfour's father.

Dessert

If it's not dessert if it's not chocolate, then **Coco's Chocolate Café** (1759 Bardstown Rd., 502/454-9810, www.cocoschocolatecafe.com, noon–9 P.M. Tues.–Wed., noon–10 P.M. Thurs., noon–11 P.M. Fri.–Sat., 3–8 P.M. Sun., $1.75–5.99) is your place. Pretty much everything here—from the color of the walls to the truffles, fondue, and mousse—is chocolate. The drinking chocolate puts regular ol' hot chocolate to shame, but if chocolate treats with chocolate drinks is too much, there's also specialty coffee.

At **Homemade Ice Cream and Pie Kitchen** (2525 and 1041 Bardstown Rd., 502/459-8184 & 502/618-3380, www.piekitchen.com, 10 A.M.–9:30 P.M. Mon.–Thurs., 10 A.M.–11 P.M. Fri.–Sat., noon–9 P.M. Sun., $2–6), they don't mislead you with their name. The scrumptious homemade ice cream, pie, and other desserts are what have kept Louisvillians coming in for over a quarter century (when what was a lunch counter became dessert heaven thanks to its oft-requested pies). The caramel iced Dutch apple pie and the seasonal pumpkin ice cream win raves, but they probably make a delicious version of whatever flavor's your favorite. If you've been really good,

reward yourself with a combo of the store's two namesake dishes: ice cream pie!

Legend has it that Elizabeth Kizito of **Kizito Cookies** (1398 Bardstown Rd., 502/456-2891, www.kizito.com, 7 A.M.–5 P.M. Tues.–Fri., 8 A.M.–5 P.M. Sat., $1.50) was born under a banana tree, then learned to bake from her father in Africa before immigrating to the United States at age 17. Whether that's true I don't know, but I do know that Kizito cookies are legendary in their own right. Big enough to share and perfectly chewy, the cookies come in 10 different flavors. Stick with traditional chocolate chip or try the pecan-and-chocolate Lucky in Kentucky; it's impossible to go wrong.

Coffee Houses

Day's Espresso & Coffee (1420 Bardstown Rd., 502/456-1170, www.dayscoffee.com, 6:30 A.M.–10 P.M. Mon.–Thurs., 6:30 A.M.–11 P.M. Fri., 7 A.M.–11 P.M. Sat., 7 A.M.–10 P.M. Sun., $2–5) claims to have the finest cappuccino in town, and customers declare the iced latte to be unbeatable. Though the crowd here is mixed, Day's is particularly welcoming to Louisville's gay community.

Heine Brothers (1449 Bardstown Rd., 502/454-5212, www.heinebroscoffee.com, 6:30 A.M.–11 P.M. Mon.–Thurs., 6:30 A.M.–midnight Fri.–Sat., 7 A.M.–11 P.M. Sun., $2–5), Louisville's neighborhood coffee shop, serves the coffee that keeps the Derby City chugging. Having co-founded a first-of-its kind organic, fair-trade, and green coffee co-op as well as a non-profit that turns coffee grounds into compost, Heine Bros. isn't just good for a pick-me-up, it's also good for your soul. Of the seven locations, the four Bardstown Road locations (1295, 2200, and 3060 Bardstown Rd.) are most popular; all, however, welcome you to bring a book, a computer, or a friend and hang out for as long as you like.

Highland Coffee (1140 Bardstown Rd., 502/451-4545, www.highlandcoffee.com, 6 A.M.–11 P.M. Mon.–Thurs., 6 A.M.–midnight Fri., 7 A.M.–11 P.M. Sat., 7 A.M.–10 P.M. Sat., $2–5), which draws a young, artsy crowd, claims to be "keeping Louisville wired," with their selection of coffee drinks and baked goods. For mid-day munchies, try their smoothies and paninis, and if you're feeling adventurous, check out their specialty menu, which offers such limited-time tastes as Kentucky bacon-maple latte.

Going beyond the usual limits of a coffee shop, **Ray's Monkey House** (1578 Bardstown Rd., 502/459-4373, www.raysmonkeyhouse.

com, 7:30 A.M.–10 P.M. Mon.–Thurs., 7:30 A.M.–11 P.M. Fri., 8:30 A.M.–11 P.M. Sat. 8:30 A.M.–10 P.M. Sun., $2–5) complements its coffee (served in recyclable cups made from cornstarch) with a vegetarian menu, a selection of beers, and live music. If you want to talk progressive ideas with people who truly care about the issues, this is your place. And oh yeah, bring the kids, who are sure to love the play area and board games.

Information and Transportation

INFORMATION

The **Louisville Visitors Center** (301 S. 4th St., 502/379-6109, www.gotolouisville.com, 10 A.M.–5 P.M. Mon.–Sat., noon–5 P.M. Sun.), conveniently located between the Kentucky International Convention Center and Fourth Street Live!, offers advice, maps, reservations, brochures, and everything else you need to arrange your visit.

If you're downtown and looking to mail a postcard home, the 4th Street **post office** (411 S. 4th St.) is most central, but it's open 9 A.M.–5 P.M. weekdays only.

The *Courier-Journal* (www.courierjournal.com), Kentucky's largest newspaper, is published daily in Louisville. *LEO Weekly* (www.leoweekly.com) is the city's alternative newspaper and the source for what's happening around town. You can pick it up free at restaurants, bars, shops, and stands around the city.

GETTING THERE
Air

Though UPS is the only carrier flying internationally from the amusingly named **Louisville International Airport** (600 Terminal Dr., 502/368-6524, www.flylouisville.com)—still referred to by many locals as Standiford Field (the former name and the source of airport code SDF)—you can't find many other faults with the airport. It's conveniently located only about five miles south of downtown, and it's notably simple

to navigate, with two terminals, each branching off from the main hall and each easily reached on foot. Airlines offer non-stop flights to 20 destinations and a slew of connecting flights to cities around the world. To get to or from the airport, you can take a taxi ($17.85 to/from downtown), rental car, hotel shuttle, or bus.

TARC Route 2 runs between downtown (stops at 5th & Market and 1st & Broadway) and the airport. On weekdays, the first departure from the airport is at 5:36 A.M. and the last departure is at 11:11 P.M.; the first departure from downtown is at 6:05 A.M. and the last is at 10:15 P.M. On Saturdays, the first departure from the airport is at 5:41 A.M. and the last departure is at 9:56 P.M.; the first departure from downtown is at 6:10 A.M. and the last is at 9:20 P.M. On Sundays, the first departure from the airport is at 7:11 A.M. and the last departure is at 9:56 P.M.; the first departure from downtown is at 6:10 A.M. and the last is at 9:20 P.M. The bus ride lasts about 30 minutes and costs $1.50. Buses depart every 50–90 minutes depending on the day and time.

Bus

Greyhound services Louisville with a downtown station (720 W. Muhammad Ali Blvd., 502/561-2805, www.greyhound.com). The station is open daily around-the-clock, except between 10 A.M. and 12:30 P.M.

© THERESA DOWELL BLACKINTON

trolley in downtown Louisville

Car

Lying at the intersections of I-65, I-64, and I-71, Louisville is easily accessed by car from north, south, east, and west.

GETTING AROUND
Car Rental

Your best bet for exploring Louisville, especially if you want to go beyond downtown, is to rent a car. Avis (800/331-1212, www.avis.com), Budget (800/527-0700, www.budget.com), Dollar (800/800-3665, www.dollar.com), Enterprise (800/261-7331, www.enterprise.com), Hertz (800/654-3131, www.hertz.com), National (877/222-9058, www.nationalcar.com), and Thrifty (888/400-8877, www.thrifty.com) all have desks at the airport. Cars can be reserved online through the companies' national websites.

Metered street parking is available downtown with limits of 1–4 hours. The meters take nickels, dimes, quarters, and dollar coins. Parking is free on the streets after 6 P.M. and on

Sundays. The city runs six lots and 13 garages that cost $3–5 for all-day parking, though rates go up for events. Look for blue PARC signs to identify these parking areas.

Bus

Public transportation within Louisville is offered by **TARC** (www.ridetarc.org), the Transit Authority of the River City, and is limited to buses and trolleys. Getting across town via bus is not a particularly efficient way of travel, but the Main–Market and Fourth Street trolleys cover nearly all of downtown's tourist sites. Use the "Plan Your Trip" feature on TARC's website to determine your options. Bus fare is $1.50 for adults, $0.75 for students, seniors, and riders with disabilities. Transfers are free. Trolley fare is $0.50 for most riders, $0.25 for seniors and riders with disabilities. A Day Tripper pass offers unlimited rides on the day of purchase for $3. Starting and stopping times for the routes vary greatly, with some routes starting as early as 4 A.M. and ending as late as midnight.

Taxi

Though it's not too difficult to flag down a taxi in the city center, it's almost always easier and safer to call and order a cab. All hotels and many restaurants and sights will arrange a taxi for you; just ask at the concierge, hostess, or information desk. Cabs in Louisville are metered with rates set by the city.

Yellow Cab (502/636-5511) has the largest fleet in town and is a reliable option around the clock. Major credit cards are accepted.

Pedicabs and Horse Trams

If you're looking for an alternative way of getting from point A to point B, hop in one of bright red vehicles operated by **Derby City Pedicabs** (502/338-0877, www.derbycity-pedicabs.com), most often found near Fourth Street Live!, Slugger Field, Waterfront Park, and along Bardstown Road. Drivers work for tips only, so you decide the fare. Don't be cheap; it's not easy to pedal passengers around town, and the drivers are all fun people.

If elegant is more your style, then opt to see downtown Louisville from an old-fashioned carriage crafted by Amish artisans and pulled by majestic draft horses on a ride with **Louisville Horse Trams** (502/581-0100, www.louisvillehorsetrams.com). A standard 15-minute ride for up to three people costs $20, with prices going up from there depending on length of trip and number of people. Reservations are recommended, though you can often find the carriages out on the town, especially on summer weekends and near Waterfront Park.

Tours

If you'd rather leave the planning up to someone else, contact **Mint Julep Tours** (866/986-8779, www.mintjuleptours.com, from $59) to sign up for their Historic Louisville Tour, which hits city highlights downtown, along the Ohio River, and in Old Louisville. They also offer more specialized tours including a Boutique Shop Hop for all you fashionistas, and a Moonshine & Madness Tour that takes you back in time to the Roarin' Twenties when Louisville was known as Sin City. Additional tours depart from Louisville and take you farther afield—to bourbon distilleries, wineries, horse farms, and other attractions around the state.

Vicinity of Louisville

For day excursions, you have a number of options. You can head southwest to Fort Knox to get a dose of military history, southeast to Taylorsville to enjoy a day at the lake, or east to Shelbyville to visit standardbred horse farms.

FORT KNOX

Located south of Louisville, Fort Knox is a city-sized army base with a population of 23,000 soldiers and civilians. As you approach, don't be surprised to hear the thunder of tanks, as Fort Knox is home to the U.S. Armor Center and School and is the training grounds for the M1 Abrams Main Battle Tank used by both the Army and the Marines. Additionally, as one of five basic combat training facilities in the nation, Fort Knox sees a constant stream of new recruits pass through its gates.

To the general public, Fort Knox is most well known as the home of the U.S. Bullion Depository, or in lay terms, the Gold Vault. Its aura of impenetrability has introduced Fort Knox into the popular vernacular, and it has appeared in many movies such as the James Bond flick *Goldfinger*. Unfortunately, without a presidential order, the vault, which contains over 5,000 tons of gold, is as inaccessible as claimed, but Fort Knox itself is open to visitors.

Sights

For military buffs, the **General George Patton**

Museum (4554 Fayette Ave., 502/624-3812, www.generalpatton.org, 9 A.M.–4:30 P.M. Mon.–Fri., 10 A.M.–4:30 P.M. Sat.–Sun., until 6 P.M. on weekends May–Sept., free) is a must-see. Established shortly after the end of World War II, the museum has two main focuses: artifacts related to General George S. Patton Jr. and mechanized cavalry and armory. Unless you're a member of the Armed Forces, you probably won't get a more up-close look at armored vehicles dating back to 1917. And for fans of Old Blood and Guts, this museum is where you come to pay tribute to the man, the myth, and the legend.

For an intense experience, visit Fort Knox on Memorial Day weekend when the Patton Museum sponsors the Life of the Soldier event, which features live re-enactments, including a mock tank battle. That's something you won't find anywhere else.

Getting There and Around

Fort Knox is located 35 miles south of Louisville, off of U.S. 31. All vehicles and visitors are subject to search, and weapons are not permitted on base.

TAYLORSVILLE LAKE

Stretching through three counties and covering 3,050 acres, Taylorsville Lake is the closest destination to Louisville for water recreation. The fishing is good here, whether you're looking to cast for bluegill and sunfish along the shore or are angling to land a bass. Skiing, swimming, and other water sports are also popular. Built in the 1960s by the U.S. Army Corps of Engineers to control flooding, Taylorsville Lake is surrounded by 12,093 acres of protected land used for wildlife management as well as recreation. Whether you wish to get out on the water or explore land-based activities, you'll want to base yourself at Taylorsville Lake State Park.

Recreation

Located right on the water, **Taylorsville Lake State Park** (2825 Overlook Rd., 502/477-8882, http://parks.ky.gov, free) draws anglers,

water skiers, personal watercraft users, and pleasure boaters looking for a day in the sun. The park maintains four boat ramps that are free and accessible to the public. If you don't have your own watercraft, the **Taylorsville Marina** (1240 Settlers Trace Rd., 502/477-8766, www.taylorsvillelakemarina.com) will set you up for the day. You can rent pontoons ($169–199), ski boats ($199), deck boats ($249), and Jon boats ($59) by the day and Jet Skis ($75) by the hour.

Beyond the lake, the park encompasses 1,200 acres of forest and field. The 16-mile trail system is a favorite for horseback riding, though it's officially a mixed-use trail also open to mountain bikers and hikers. During wet periods, the horses can really tear up the trail, so if you're looking to hike, check conditions before you lace up your boots. The trails are particularly nice in autumn when the trees are ablaze with color and the weather is mild.

Accommodations

Edgewater Resort (1238 Settlers Trace Rd., 866/641-3343, www.edgewatertaylorsville-lake.com, $199–249), the only development on Taylorsville Lake, offers fully furnished cottages complete with decks with hot tubs. The majority of the cottages sleep four, though some can accommodate up to eight guests—perfect for a family vacation. From the cottages, a series of paths provide access to the lake, while boaters can launch their craft from a nearby ramp. A beach area has been created for resort guests, and Edgewater also offers trail bikes, canoe rentals, and guided boat excursions.

Geared toward RV campers, the **Taylorsville Lake Campground** (1320 Park Rd., 502/477-8713, http://parks.ky.gov, $17–25) is open year-round and has 42 large sites with full hook-ups. In a nod to the park's popularity with horse lovers, 10 additional sites are designated for horse camping. All campers share a central service building that includes laundry facilities.

Food

Aside from a selection of pizza, sandwiches, and burgers sold at the Taylorsville Marina, no food vendors operate in the park. Bring what you need with you or stock up at **Settler's Trace Grocery & Deli** (25 Overlook Rd., 502/477-9676, 5 A.M.–8 P.M. Mon.–Sat., 7 A.M.–7 P.M. Sun.), which is right up the road from the marina.

Getting There and Around

Taylorsville Lake State Park is located about 30 miles southeast of the intersection of I-265 and I-64. From Louisville, take eastbound I-64 to Taylorsville Road (Exit 32A) and then follow signs to the lake and park entrances.

SHELBYVILLE

Known as the Saddlebred Capital of the World, Shelbyville is to equestrian events what Lexington is to thoroughbred horse farms. In fact, the eminence of the Shelbyville horse farms helped Kentucky land the 2010 World Equestrian Games, an international competition that had never before taken place outside of Europe.

Beyond its horse farms, Shelbyville is a friendly small town with a center that begs you to get out of your car and explore it on foot. Main Street and Washington Street are particularly pedestrian friendly with a slew of storefronts selling antiques, art, and home decor.

Sights

Though none of Shelbyville's American saddlebred horse farms have regularly scheduled hours for visits from the public, the **Shelbyville Visitors Bureau** (800/680-6388, tours@shelbyvilleky.com) organizes tours of a working farm. Tours last 60–90 minutes and occur year-round, though you'll need to make reservations two or three days ahead of your visit. If you stay at a local hotel, the tour is free, and your hotel can help with the arrangements. For those not overnighting in Shelbyville, tours cost $6 for adults and $3 for youth 5–12. If it works with your schedule, aim for a morning tour, as that's when the horses will be going through their workouts.

For a taste (both literal and figurative) of farm life, locals swear that there's not a better place in the area than **Gallrein Farms** (1029 Vigo Rd., 502/633-4849, www.gallreinfarms. com, 9 A.M.–5 P.M. Mon.–Sat., 1–5 P.M. Sun.), especially if you have kids. The owners and staff are fond of children, tailoring the farm to them, and are happy to let them run and explore. The farm is open spring through fall, and contains a produce market, as well as a petting zoo and duck pond loved by both the young and the young at heart. Spring and summer offer berry picking, while fall is particularly popular thanks to horse-drawn wagon rides, pumpkin picking, and a corn maze.

Shopping

Antiques hunters seek out Shelbyville's **Wakefield-Scearce Galleries** (525 Washington St., 502/633-4382, www.wakefieldscearce.com, 10 A.M.–5 P.M. Mon.–Sat.), which has 32,000 square feet of showrooms dedicated to English antiques. Even if you aren't in the market for any of the amazing pieces on sale here, stop in to browse the impressive collection of antique silver, paintings, furniture, and other home accessories.

Recreation

Favored by bass anglers, the 325-acre **Guist Creek Lake** (11990 Boat Dock Rd., 502/647-5359, www.guistcreek.com, $5 launch fee) also contains catfish, crappie, and bluegill, and it's a rare day when you can't find a quiet spot to cast your line. For those without their own boat, 14-foot Jon boats are available for rent at the marina, which also stocks tackle, boat gear, fuel, food, and drinks. From the end of May to the end of September, water skiing is allowed in a specially designated area. For those who like to do some night fishing or who want to make a weekend of it, a campground is open March–November with both tent ($15) and pull-through ($18) sites.

Accommodations

Many people visit Shelbyville on a day trip and spend the night in either Louisville or Frankfort, since the options in Shelbyville are limited. The usual chain hotel suspects do exist, however, with the **Ramada** (251 Breighton Circle, 502/633-9933, www.ramada.com, $79–199) the best of the bunch. Built in 2006, the Ramada has large, clean, modern rooms as well as a fitness center and indoor pool.

In nearby Simpsonville, which lies between Louisville and Shelbyville, the **Yellow Carriage House** (4876 Shelbyville Rd., 502/376-9257, www.yellowcarriagehouse.com, $159) is a secluded bed-and-breakfast surrounded by horse fields. Choose between the King and Queen suites in the main house, each with marble shower and a private balcony or veranda, or elect for the separate Carriage House, where the candlelight breakfast available to all guests is delivered straight to your room on a silver platter.

Food

Turns out it wasn't just the Colonel who could cook. At ◖ **Claudia Sanders Dinner House** (3202 Shelbyville Rd., 502/633-5600, www.claudiasanders.com, 11 A.M.–9 P.M. Tues.–Sun., $9.25–18.95), you can choose from a long list of Kentucky specialties straight from the cookbook of Mrs. Colonel Sanders. Though fried chicken and country ham take up a prime portion of the menu, you can also select steaks, chops, fish, and seafood, as well as salads and sandwiches. Dinner is served family style with unlimited vegetable side dishes and a bread bowl that never empties, and of course, all meals are served with a heavy helping of Southern hospitality.

For a pick-me-up, stop in at **Sixth and Main Coffee House** (547 Main St., 502/647-7751, www.6amcoffee.com, 6 A.M.–6 P.M. Mon.–Sat., 8 A.M.–1 P.M. Sun., $1.95–4.35), where the brightly colored walls and expertly brewed coffee drinks will get you going again. If you'd rather relax, grab a book from the shelf running the length of the café or just watch out the window as small town life occurs.

Get friendly with the locals at the monthly **Lake Shelby Fish Fry** (717 Burks Branch Rd., 502/633-5059, www.shelbycountyparks.com), held 5:30–8 P.M. on the third Friday of the month May–September. For $8.50, you'll get a heaping plate of fish, coleslaw, hush puppies, and potato wedges, as well as ice cream for dessert and your choice of tea or lemonade. The conversation is free.

Not quite in town but just a few miles away, Simpsonville's **Old Stone Inn** (6905 Shelbyville Rd., 502/722-8200, www.old-stone-inn.com, lunch 11 A.M.–2 P.M.Thurs.–Fri., dinner 4–10 P.M. Mon.–Sat., $14–27) is worth the trip. This limestone building from the early 1800s has seen life as a stagecoach stop as well as a tavern and inn, though it's been operating as a restaurant since 1920. Enjoy the warm ambiance created by the four original fireplaces, while feasting on elegantly plated Southern favorites like country ham, shrimp and grits, and chicken livers. When the weather's nice, take advantage of happy hour on the patio complete with live local music.

Getting There and Around

From Louisville, Shelbyville is an easy 30-mile drive straight east on I-64. You can continue east on I-64 to both Frankfort (about 30 miles) and Lexington (about 60 miles).

BARDSTOWN, THE BOURBON TRAIL, AND FRANKFORT

The spirit of Kentucky flows out of the central region that includes Bardstown, the Bourbon Trail, and Frankfort. For some this spirit is religious. Bardstown is Kentucky's holy land, home to the first Catholic diocese in the West. Today multiple religious orders base themselves here, and landmark religious sites draw the faithful. For many more, however, the spirit they think of when the towns of this region spring to mind is amber colored and comes in a bottle. Here in central Kentucky, the world's best bourbon—America's only native spirit—is distilled, bottled, and aged.

The locations featured in this chapter are not cities; they're towns. Even Frankfort, the unassuming capital of Kentucky, is no more than a large town. You can explore each and every destination on foot, strolling down revitalized Main Streets lined with historic buildings hosting restaurants, B&Bs, and shops as you make your way from site to site. Expect people to say hello, to ask where you're from, to point out their favorite places. This is small town America, where festivals are still begun with parades, where neighbors are never strangers, and where the best cooking is home cooking.

Leave each of the towns that dot the route between Bardstown and Frankfort, and you'll find yourself amidst farmland. The limestone layer that makes the water so fine for bourbon is good for growing things too. Weathered barns, tall silos, bright green fields, and large herds of cattle or other livestock enhance the scenery as you travel from distillery to distillery. Many of the distilleries themselves are located essentially on farmland, the warehouses

© THERESA DOWELL BLACKINTON

HIGHLIGHTS

🌙 **My Old Kentucky Home State Park:** Take a tour of the Federal-style home that inspired Stephen Foster to write what would become Kentucky's state song (page 78).

🌙 **Civil War Museum:** Though small, this museum on Bardstown's Museum Row has important collections and does a good job of using its artifacts to convey the story of the Civil War (page 79).

🌙 **Kentucky Bourbon Festival:** A must for bourbon aficionados, the festival allows you to meet master distillers, sip premium bourbons, and celebrate American's native spirit (page 81).

🌙 **Bernheim Arboretum:** Immerse yourself in the natural beauty of Central Kentucky while hiking, fishing, or admiring a variety of gardens (page 90).

🌙 **Maker's Mark Distillery:** Watch as workers hand dip bottles of Maker's Mark in the signature red wax on a tour of this idyllic distillery (page 92).

🌙 **Thomas D. Clark Center for Kentucky History:** Trace the history of Kentucky back through thousands of years by way of interactive exhibits and well-done performances (page 101).

🌙 **Buffalo Trace Distillery:** Passionate guides make for an excellent tour that con-

LOOK FOR 🌙 TO FIND RECOMMENDED SIGHTS, ACTIVITIES, DINING, AND LODGING.

cludes with a tasting of your choice of spirits (page 102).

where barrels of bourbon age easy to pick out once you know what you're looking for.

One of the most idyllic regions of Kentucky, as well as the area that is attracting the most new tourists, Bardstown, the Bourbon Trail, and Frankfort are where you go to taste Kentucky's spirit.

PLANNING YOUR TIME

For a satisfying taste of the region, you need to give yourself at minimum a four-day weekend. Spend the first day in Bardstown, visiting the distilleries there and in nearby Clermont.

Fill any free time with visits to Bardstown's historic and religious sites. For the next two days, dedicate yourself to enjoying the small towns along the Bourbon Trail—Loretto, Lebanon, and Lawrenceburg. End your trip in Frankfort, where you can fill up on Kentucky history and then finish your Bourbon Trail adventure at Buffalo Trace Distillery. (Although, actually, to do the entire Bourbon Trail, you also need to go to Versailles, which is near Lexington, to visit Woodford Reserve.) Those without an interest in bourbon could still follow this same path, enjoying the scenery and

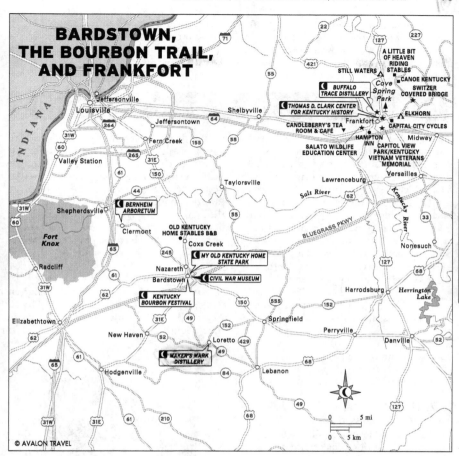

BARDSTOWN, THE BOURBON TRAIL, AND FRANKFORT

BARDSTOWN

substituting historical and cultural attractions for distilleries. This route—Clermont, Bardstown, Loretto, Lebanon, Lawrenceburg, Frankfort (and Versailles)—makes the most sense if you are starting from Louisville. If you're starting from Lexington, you can simply flip the route.

To really immerse yourself in this region of Central Kentucky, give yourself a week. You could fit each of the towns in this section into your itinerary with that amount of time, or you could spend a more leisurely time in the towns that interest you the most. Add Hodgenville

and Springfield with their many Lincoln attractions to the agenda, and get outdoors either by hiking the Millennium Trail in Bernheim Forest or by paddling with Canoe Kentucky.

If your primary goal is to make it to each of the area's distilleries, you could schedule your trip in two days. You'd have to be meticulous about your itinerary, however, as distilleries offer tours only at set times. You'll also want to pay attention to day of the week, as some distilleries are closed one day a week, most often on Sunday. Time of year is also crucial when planning a distillery-based trip.

Tour schedules are more limited in winter, but those with a real interest in the distillation process will also want to avoid summer, since many of the distilleries go into shutdown during the hottest months. You can still tour the facilities and taste the goods, but you won't see the process in action. Spring and fall are ideal.

Bardstown

The second oldest town in Kentucky, Bardstown, at first impression, feels a bit like it belongs in the Northeast. Remarkable Federal-style homes line the major thoroughfares, which meet at a traffic circle in which the courthouse sits. Historic markers are chock a block, pointing out the importance of building after building. But take a moment to get to know the town, and you'll realize it's definitively Kentucky. My Old Kentucky Home, the landmark chosen to represent Kentucky on the state quarter, is located here after all. So is Heaven Hill distillery, the first Catholic cathedral in the West, one of the nation's best Civil War museums, and a slew of restaurants that know how to fry chicken. In Bardstown you'll find all the components that make this region notable—bourbon sites, religious sites, and historical sites—making it a great starting point for a trip along the Bourbon Trail.

BOURBON TRAIL SIGHTS
Heaven Hill Distillery
Built of limestone and copper, two elements important to bourbon making, the Bourbon Heritage Center at Heaven Hill Distillery (1311 Gilkey Run Rd., 502/337-1000, www. bourbonheritagecenter.com, 10 A.M.–5 P.M. Tues.–Sat., free admission and tour) is an attractive building loaded with museum-quality exhibits on the history of bourbon. Learn about the accidental father of bourbon and how bourbon got its name before joining one of the tours. The 1.5-hour deluxe tour includes two films, an in-depth narration of bourbon history and bourbon production, and a visit to the warehouse, and ends with a tasting of Evan Williams and Elijah Craig bourbons. The tasting, which takes place in the barrel-shaped

tasting room, is very professionally done, focusing not just on taste, but also on color and nose. Those with a bourbon obsession might want to consider the three-hour Behind the Scenes Tour ($25), which turns participants into true bourbon experts. Tours depart on the hour, with the last tour scheduled for one hour prior to close. Tours are also offered on Sundays March–December, but local law forbids sales and tastings on Sunday.

Tom Moore Distillery
A tour of Tom Moore Distillery (300 Barton Rd., 502/348-3774, 9:30 A.M. and 1:30 P.M. Mon.–Fri., free tour) is very much a factory tour, requiring the use of safety goggles at

the world's largest bourbon barrel, at Tom Moore Distillery

© THERESA DOWELL BLACKINTON

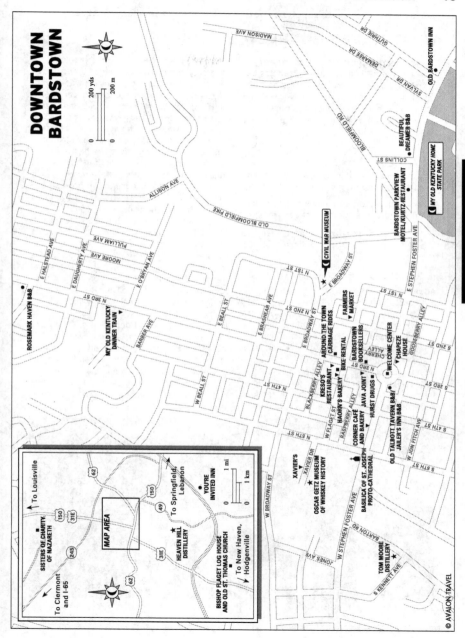

BARDSTOWN

DOWNTOWN BARDSTOWN

200 yds
200 m

© AVALON TRAVEL

WHAT MAKES BOURBON BOURBON?

Remember in geometry class when you learned that all squares are rectangles but not all rectangles are squares? Well bourbon is just like that. All bourbons are whiskeys but not all whiskeys are bourbons. For a whiskey to be a bourbon whiskey, it must meet a very specific set of criteria.

- It must be made with at least 51 percent corn.

- It must consist of only grain, yeast, and water. No color or flavor can be added.

- It must be aged in brand new charred white oak barrels for a minimum of two years.

- It must be distilled to no more than 160 proof and barreled at no more than 125 proof.

- It must be bottled at no less than 80 proof.

Additionally, as America's only native spirit, bourbon must be distilled in the United States. Though technically, it can be distilled anywhere in the country, 95 percent of the world's bourbon comes from Kentucky. Two things in particular make Kentucky an ideal place to produce bourbon. The first is the abundance of limestone springs, which give off water that is rich in nutrients but free of flavor. The second is that Kentucky has four very distinct seasons. When bourbon enters the barrel, it is a clear liquid not all that different from moonshine. When it exits the barrel, it is an amber-colored liquid rich with flavors that range from vanilla to spice to caramel to butterscotch. All of bourbon's color and flavor comes from the charred white oak barrel. The charring brings out the sugars in the wood, which the bourbon then absorbs through a process of expanding into the barrel during hot Kentucky summers and then contracting out of it in cold winters. Different varieties of bourbon are produced through both alterations in the recipe and changes in the amount of time the bourbon ages.

Now about the name bourbon. Many residents of and visitors to Kentucky think that Bourbon County was named for the drink, whereas, in fact, the drink was named for the county (which was named for the French royal family). Once an enormous county, Bourbon County was home to the Ohio River port from which barrels of Kentucky corn whiskey were shipped out to the rest of the country. As the barrels were loaded onto boats, they were stamped with the word "Bourbon" to indicate their port of origin. As Kentucky whiskey gained a following, people began to refer to the liquor as bourbon thanks to the stamp on the barrel. The name stuck, and the best whiskey in the world has been known as bourbon ever since.

© THERESA DOWELL BLACKINTON

sample of bourbon at Buffalo Trace Distillery

times. When the distillery is operating, you'll witness everything from the receipt of grains to the fermentation process to bottling. You may even get a look at the quality control process, in which the bourbons undergo stringent lab tests. Other tour activities include a visit to the spring from which the distillery gets its water as well as a stop at the world's largest bourbon barrel. Unfortunately, Tom Moore is not licensed, as of this writing, to give samples.

Oscar Getz Museum of Whiskey History

Bourbon and whiskey aficionados can't miss the Oscar Getz Museum of Whiskey History (114 N. 5th St., 502/348-2999, www.whiskeymuseum.com, 10 A.M.–5 P.M. Mon.–Fri., 10 A.M.–4 P.M. Sat., noon–4 P.M. Sun. May–Oct., 10 A.M.–4 P.M. Tues.–Sat., noon–4 P.M. Sun. Nov.–Apr., free admission), which bursts with whiskey-related paraphernalia. You'll find clever advertising art, moonshine stills, Abraham Lincoln's liquor license, antique distilling vessels, and more. The museum, which is a bit tricky to find, is located in Spalding Hall on the St. Joe campus and shares space with the **Bardstown Historical Museum,** a single hall filled with items related to local history.

RELIGIOUS SIGHTS
Basilica of St. Joseph Proto-Cathedral

In 1808, Pope Pius VII created the Diocese of Bardstown, the first Catholic diocese in the West, with jurisdiction over Kentucky, Tennessee, and the entire Northwest Territory. In order to formalize Bardstown's position, Bishop Flaget oversaw the creation of St. Joseph (301 W. Stephen Foster Ave., 502/348-3126, www.stjoechurch.com), a majestic cathedral built from bricks baked on the grounds and poplar trees cut from nearby forests and decorated with artwork donated by European royalty. In 1841, when the diocese moved to Louisville, St. Joseph's became a parish church, but as the first cathedral built in the West, it received the name St. Joseph's Proto-

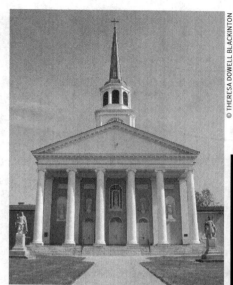

Basilica of St. Joseph Proto-Cathedral

Cathedral. In 2001, it was honored with the title of basilica, one of only two in the state. Though you're welcome to explore the basilica on your own, it's best to take advantage of the guided tours, which provide insight into the construction and history of the church as well as the magnificent artwork adorning it. Tours are available on a walk-in basis 9 A.M.–5 P.M. Monday–Friday, 9 A.M.–3 P.M. Saturday, and 1–5 P.M. Sunday April–October. Tours, which may be canceled due to special services, are free, though donations are welcome.

Bishop Flaget Log House and Old St. Thomas Church

The first permanent residence of the first bishop of the West, the Bishop Flaget Log House (870 St. Thomas Ln., 502/348-3717, www.st-thomasparish.org) is considered the oldest structure associated with Catholicism in the Midwest. The restored home is set up to represent the year 1812, when the log building served as a seminary. Old St. Thomas Church, consecrated in 1816 and renovated in 2006, is still the parish home of an active community of Catholics, and visitors are welcome to attend Mass at the church. Tours of the log house are conducted by appointment.

Sisters of Charity of Nazareth

Founded at the Bishop Flaget Log House in 1812 by Mother Catherine Spalding, the Sisters of Charity of Nazareth (Nazareth Rd., 502/348-1500, www.scnfamily.org, 9 A.M.–4 P.M. Mon.–Sat., 1–4 P.M. Sun.) now work in 17 states as well as in Belize, Botswana, India, and Nepal. On a visit to their Nazareth campus, you can watch a short video detailing the good work the sisters do around the world, become acquainted with their heritage in the history room, attend services at St. Vincent, and chat with members of the order. You're also free to explore the manicured grounds, which are graced with many quiet spots ideal for reflection. Additionally, the sisters offer a full schedule of guided spiritual retreats as well as accommodation for private retreatants.

quiet spot for contemplation on the campus of the Sisters of Charity of Nazareth

HISTORIC SIGHTS
◖ My Old Kentucky Home State Park

Federal Hill, the home of the distinguished Rowan Family, has, thanks to Stephen Foster and the song he penned while visiting the home in 1852, become known to generations as My Old Kentucky Home. The three-story brick house is the centerpiece of My Old Kentucky Home State Park (501 E. Stephen Foster Ave., 502/348-3502, http://parks.ky.gov, 9 A.M.–4:45 P.M. daily Mar.–Dec.; Thurs.–Sun. only Jan.–Feb.), and costumed tour guides lead visitors through the house, doling out information and anecdotes about family history and the artifacts in the home. An impressive 75 percent of the items in the house, which is decorated in the style of the mid-1800s, actually belonged to the Rowan family. Tours of the house cost $5.50 for adults, $5 for seniors, and $3.50 for youth 6–12, but visitors to the park are welcome to stroll the grounds, visit the family cemetery, and picnic on the beautifully landscaped lawn free of charge. A designated picnic area with tables, a covered pavilion, and a playground is located on Loretto Road. The park also includes a golf course and campground.

Historic Walking Tour

Ask for a copy of the Historic Walking Tour brochure at the Welcome Center (1 Court Sq., 502/348-4877), or download it from the tourism website (www.visitbardstown.com); then set out on a 48-stop tour. All sites are within a three-block radius of Court Square. While the brochure gives cursory information on each site, many sites also have informative signs placed in front relaying information about architecture and history.

OTHER SIGHTS
Museum Row

Made up of five distinct museums, each of which can be visited individually or as part of a package, Museum Row (310 E. Broadway, 502/349-0291, www.civil-war-museum.org, 10 A.M.–5 P.M. daily Mar.–Dec. 15) focuses primarily on history. A three-museum combo

My Old Kentucky Home State Park

ticket is available for $8.50 for adults and $4 for youth; a five-museum combo ticket costs $10 for adults and $4 for youth.

CIVIL WAR MUSEUM

The most significant of the five museums and a must-see is the Civil War Museum ($6 adults, $2 youth 7–12), which has been named the fourth best museum of its type by *North & South,* the official magazine of the Civil War Society. The museum focuses on the action that took place in the Civil War's Western theater (Kentucky, Tennessee, Mississippi, Georgia, and the Carolinas) and portrays the war from both Union and Confederate perspectives. The outer exhibit tells the chronological history of battles while the inner exhibit focuses on more detailed stories, with authentic artifacts illustrating the information. The artifacts on hand are most impressive and include flags, uniforms, weaponry, personal and medical kits, and more, much of which belonged to generals and other high-ranking officers.

WOMEN'S CIVIL WAR MUSEUM

Complementing the Civil War Museum is the Women's Civil War Museum ($4 adults, $2 youth), which documents the many ways in which women contributed to the war effort, from acting as nurses, spies, and even soldiers, to stepping up to fill roles at home and in the factory.

THE WAR MEMORIAL OF MID AMERICA MUSEUM

The War Memorial of Mid America Museum ($4 adults, $2 youth) is the final military-themed attraction on Museum Row. This museum presents artifacts from the Revolutionary War through Desert Storm and tells the story of those who have fought in defense of the United States, with special attention paid to local men and women.

PIONEER VILLAGE

Representing the oldest era of regional history, the Pioneer Village ($4 adults, $2 youth) strives to authentically re-create a 1790s village. The cabins come from the local area and date back over 200 years. On the third Saturday of each month, re-enactors populate the village, offering blacksmithing, weaving, and

KENTUCKY'S STATE SONG

Every year on Derby Day, as the contenders in America's most prestigious horse race head to the post, the crowd stands for the singing of "My Old Kentucky Home." And without fail, this simple song by Stephen Foster, America's first great composer, brings tears to the eyes of men, women, boys, girls, and jockeys alike. Don't be the only one who doesn't know the words.

My Old Kentucky Home

The sun shines bright on my old Kentucky home
Tis summer, the children are gay
The corn top's ripe and the meadow's in the bloom
While the birds make music all the day
The young folks roll on the little cabin floor
All merry, all happy and bright
By 'n' by hard times come a-knocking at the door
Then my old Kentucky home goodnight
Weep no more, my lady
Oh, weep no more today
We will sing one song for the old Kentucky home
For the old Kentucky home far away

– Stephen Foster

broom-making demonstrations and providing information on daily life in frontier America.

WILDLIFE MUSEUM

The final museum in the group, the Wildlife Museum ($4 adults, $2 youth) focuses on natural history, displaying professionally stuffed animals of North America in natural-like settings. The preservation is top-notch and the displays are attention grabbing, especially the one depicting wolves in pursuit of an elk.

ENTERTAINMENT AND EVENTS
Nightlife

Freestanding bars are uncommon in Bardstown and definitely not where the action is. Instead, locals and visitors alike seek out restaurant bars for a drink and evening entertainment. The **Bourbon Bar at Old Talbott Tavern** (107 W. Stephen Foster Ave., 502/348-3494, www.talbotts.com, 4–9 P.M. Mon.–Wed., 4 P.M.–1 A.M. Thurs.–Sat., 1–8 P.M. Sun.) is a popular gathering place with (loud) live music, and the bar at **Xavier's** (112 Xavier Dr., 502/349-1116, 5–10 P.M. Tues.–Thurs., 5 P.M.–midnight Fri.–Sat.) attracts a young professional crowd with its cozy atmosphere.

Performing Arts

The Stephen Foster Story (Drama Dr., 502/348-5971, www.stephenfoster.com) is Bardstown's signature performance, drawing big crowds every summer with its song-and dance-filled story of America's first great composer. Unless it rains, the evening performances take place at the large outdoor theater on the grounds of My Old Kentucky Home State Park. In addition to putting on the classic *Stephen Foster Story,* the Stephen Foster Productions company rounds out the schedule with other musical performance. For instance, the 2010 schedule featured *Floyd Collins,* the story of a legendary Kentucky cave explorer, and *Footloose,* an adaptation of the 1984 movie. The season runs mid-June–mid-August, and tickets cost $18–23 for adults and $10–12 for youth 6–12. Fanatics should invest in the $50 pass, which allows unlimited attendance to all three musicals scheduled for the season.

Live Music

The **Live at the Park Concert Series** (502/348-5971, www.stephenfoster.com) brings popular (but sometimes dated) musicians to town to perform at the stage at My Old Kentucky Home State Park. Past performers include Davy Jones of the Monkees, the Lovin' Spoonful, Beatles tribute bands, and country musician Chuck Wicks. Tickets average about $25; those interested in multiple shows should consider purchasing season tickets, which are good for the concerts as well as the Stephen Foster Story productions.

Music lovers will also want to avail themselves of the free **Summer Band Concerts,** which are held 7–9 P.M. every Friday from Memorial Day to Labor Day in the Bardstown Community Park (E. Halstead Ave., www.cityofbardstown.org). Bands and genres change every week, so pack a picnic and make it a recurring date.

Festivals and Events
◖ KENTUCKY BOURBON FESTIVAL
For six days in mid-September, the Bourbon Capital of the World hosts the Kentucky Bourbon Festival (800/638-4877, www.kybourbonfestival.com), an absolute must for lovers of America's native spirit. Highlights of the festival include the Great Kentucky Bourbon Tasting and Gala and the Kentucky Bourbon All-Star Sampler. Each of these events allows participants to meet with master distillers and taste the best bourbons being made. Though much of the schedule is filled with events directly related to bourbon (demonstrations, seminars, tastings, and more), you'll also find golf tournaments, fun runs, art festivals, concerts, and other types of entertainment to keep you satisfied between sips.

BARDSTOWN ARTS, CRAFTS, & ANTIQUES FAIR
Nearly 200 artists and crafts people descend on Bardstown on the second weekend of October for the Bardstown Arts, Crafts, & Antiques Fair (www.visitbardstown.com), held on the streets of downtown. Shop for jewelry, pottery, woodwork, photography, prints, and more while enjoying music and local food.

SHOPPING
North Third Street is lined with shops selling gifts, apparel, and local souvenirs, so window

shop as you walk, popping in whenever something catches your eye. At **Bardstown Booksellers** (129 N. 3rd St., 502/348-1256, 9 A.M.–5:30 P.M. Mon.–Sat.), books about Kentucky fill the most prominent shelves, so it's a great place to shop if you're looking for a cookbook of traditional recipes or a coffee table book of beautiful photos. The store also stocks locally made crafts, jewelry, and food, including a mouthwatering selection of truffles, as well as popular and antiquarian books.

Old-fashioned **Hurst Drugs** (102 N. 3rd St., 502/348-9261, 8 A.M.–5:30 P.M. Mon.–Fri., 9 A.M.–4:30 P.M. Sat.) stocks a broad selection of Kentucky souvenirs, including Derby glasses, U of L and UK themed gifts, pottery, and Kentucky Proud food products. You're also welcome to have a seat at one of the red stools at the counter and enjoy a shake, malt, float, or soda.

SPORTS AND RECREATION
Golf
The **Kenny Rapier Golf Course** (668 Loretto Rd., 502/349-6542, http://parks.ky.gov, Apr.–Oct.), which is part of My Old Kentucky Home State Park, is an 18-hole, par-71 course. It was awarded four stars by *Golf Digest* in 2009 after a redesign that updated the original 1928 course to a more modern style.

Biking
Bardstown is a fun city to explore on two wheels, thanks to courteous drivers and the close proximity of attractions to each other. Cruiser-style bikes (108 W. Flaget, 502/510-1674, $15) can be rented for three-hour periods and come with map, helmet, lock, and basket.

Water Sports
Get paddling with the help of **Central Kentucky Canoe & Kayak** (502/345-9220, www.kycanoe.com), an outfitter that organizes half-day, full-day, and overnight trips for all skill levels on various waterways in the Central Kentucky area including Sympson Lake, Salt River, and Brashears Creek. Moonlight floats are particularly delightful, allowing

participants to experience the water at night. Reservations should be made in advance for all trips.

ACCOMMODATIONS
$50-100

Bardstown Parkview Motel (418 E. Stephen Foster Ave., 502/348-5983, www.bardstown-parkview.com, $60–100) doesn't claim to offer all the amenities of new hotels but instead preserves the style that made motels popular in the first place. Service at this family-owned place is friendly, the grounds are nicely manicured, and a courtyard area with pool is popular with families. Though a bit dated, rooms and suites (which have desks and cook tops) are clean and come with Internet connections. The location directly across the street from My Old Kentucky Home can't be beat. Breakfast isn't anything to write home about, but the toast, cereal, and coffee will at least get you started.

The 33 units at **Old Bardstown Inn** (510 E. Stephen Foster Ave., 502/349-0776, www.angelfire.com/ky3/oldbardstowninn, $55) offer standard motel amenities with clean rooms, each with two queen beds, wireless Internet access, and refrigerators. A continental breakfast is served in the lobby, and a pool provides a welcome escape on hot summer days. Leave your car in the lot and just cross the street to visit My Old Kentucky Home or play a round of golf.

The five rooms at **Old Talbott Tavern Bed and Breakfast** (107 W. Stephen Foster Ave., 502/348-3494, www.talbotts.com, $69–109) are named for famous Tavern guests: Abraham Lincoln, Generals Clark and Patton, Anton Heinrich, Daniel Boone, and Washington Irving. All rooms are furnished with period antiques, such as claw-foot tubs and canopy beds, but contain modern (but worn) amenities like private bath, refrigerator, and TV. Beware that the rooms can be very noisy due to both street traffic and the music played in the bar below. Breakfast is disappointing, especially considering the B&B is part of a restaurant.

You're Invited Inn (1415 Ed Brent St., 502/349-0964, www.bbonline.com, $90–110) offers guests a choice of four spacious rooms, each of which features a king bed, comfy chair or loveseat, table, microwave, refrigerator, and a basket full of snacks and teas. Choose the red room for private access to the poolside deck as well as a large bathroom with a soaker tub and separate shower. Mingle with other guests or friendly hosts Easter and Alvin in the living room, or borrow one of the nearly 1,500 DVDs on offer and relax in your room. The breakfast, which you can enjoy in the dining room or have brought to your room, will keep you full all day: a starter (hope for the piña colada–style fruit), eggs, meat, potatoes, bread, and a "dessert" of chocolate pancakes or apricot French toast. Though You're Invited Inn feels like it's in the country, it's really just a five-minute drive from the center of Bardstown, making it a great stay for those who want the best of both worlds.

$100-150

At the **Jailer's Inn Bed and Breakfast** (111 W. Stephen Foster Ave., 502/348-5551, www.jailersinn.com, $90–145), you don't have to break any laws to spend the night in the slammer. While the back jail remains preserved, the front jail has been renovated to contain six guest rooms. Five feel like typical B&B rooms, while one room, decorated in black and white and with the original bunks, maintains the aura of a jail cell. Plenty of ghost stories surround the jail, so a stay here might not be for the faint of heart.

Book a room at **Old Kentucky Home Stables Bed and Breakfast** (115 Samuels Rd., Cox's Creek, 502/349-0408, www.okhs-bb.com, $115), located 10 minutes from downtown Bardstown, and you'll be spending the night at America's oldest continuously operating saddlebred horse farm. The pre–Civil War home, with original plank floors and double-sided brick fireplace, offers large rooms with all the modern amenities, including whirlpool tubs and cable TV. Views stretch far and wide over rural countryside, and are only occasionally interrupted by a peacock strutting past,

Jailer's Inn, a former jail turned B&B

feathers spread. Owner Frankie is a history and horse buff and can ply you with trivia or spin a good story. You can also arrange riding lessons with him, though be aware that the saddlebreds he breeds, trains, and shows are big, powerful animals, not ponies.

$150-200

Named for one of Stephen Foster's songs, **Beautiful Dreamer Bed and Breakfast** (440 E. Stephen Foster Ave., 502/348-4004, www.bdreamerbb.com, $149–179) sits on property that was once part of My Old Kentucky Home. Now a street divides it from this landmark, but you can still enjoy a view of the park from the second-floor veranda. The four spacious bedrooms have large bathrooms, flat-screen TVs, reclining chairs, and big beds. Decor is clean and classic, and the walls are painted in shades of rich wine, forest green, and Kentucky blue. Breakfast is served family style, and drinks and snacks, along with games and DVDs, are available on the second-floor landing. If you have questions about the Stephen Foster Story, which you can walk to

from the B&B, just ask host Lynell. She's seen the show over 200 times!

Don't let the gas station near the entrance to **Rosemark Haven Bed and Breakfast** (714 N. 3rd St., 502/348-8218, www.rosemarkhaven.com, $139–189) intimidate you. Follow the drive back, and you'll find an impressive house located on serene grounds. Seven very large rooms, each fitted with either a fireplace or a whirlpool tub (one room has both), are located in the main house, which dates back to the 1820s and impresses with its spiral staircase and brilliant chandeliers. Families may be interested in an eighth option, the Federal House, a completely separate structure with two bedrooms, a shared bathroom, and living and dining spaces. A tobacco barn on the property has been converted into a wine bar that is open Thursday–Saturday and makes for a popular spot to socialize. If you'd rather have a quiet night, grab a DVD and retreat to your stylish room until it's time for breakfast, served every morning at 9 A.M. in the double parlor. Be sure to check the B&B policies before booking, as a number of rules, some unexpected, are enforced at the property.

Campgrounds

My Old Kentucky Home State Park hosts a campground (Loretto Rd., 502/348-3502, http://parks.ky.gov, $22), offering 39 improved sites for RVs and a separate grassy area for tent campers. Showers and restrooms are located in a central building.

FOOD
My Old Kentucky Dinner Train

Take your dinner in a vintage 1940s dinner car while enjoying a ride through the countryside on My Old Kentucky Dinner Train (N. 3rd St., 502/348-7300, www.rjcorman.com, $74.95 dinner trip, $59.95 lunch trip). During the 2.5-hour trip, a four-course dinner is served. It starts with Kentucky beer cheese; is followed by a Golden Spike salad; continues with a choice of beef, chicken, pork, fish, or vegetarian entrée; and ends with a selection of desserts. Lunch excursions offer lighter fare served over three courses. The train runs year-round, though there are more departures during summer months. Visit the website to view the schedule and make reservations.

The Chapeze House Kentucky Bourbon Cooking School

Learn to cook an entire menu of delicious foods that feature bourbon at the Kentucky Bourbon Cooking School at Chapeze House (107 E. Stephen Foster Ave., 502/507-8338, www.chapezehouse.com), run by renowned hosts Colonel Michael and Margaret Sue Masters. After helping to prepare each of the dishes, the class gets to sit down and enjoy the meal, which is served with complementary cocktails.

Farmers Market

Pick up crisp veggies, juicy fruits, and other farm-fresh products at the Farmers Market (N. 2nd and E. Flaget Sts., 7:30 A.M.–12:30 P.M. Tues., Fri., and Sat. May–Oct.), held three times a week in a permanent building in downtown Bardstown.

Cafés and Bakeries

For a healthy but delicious lunch, choose the bright and cheery **Corner Café and Bakery** (216 W. Stephen Foster Ave., 502/349-3144, 9 A.M.–3 P.M. Mon.–Fri., 10 A.M.–2 P.M. Sun., $6.99–10.95), where the wraps, sandwiches, and salads are made with organic produce and Boar's Head meats. Vegetarians will find options here, as well as a kitchen that can accommodate special requests.

If you've got a hankering for a pastry or other baked goodie, head to **Hadorn's Bakery** (118 W. Flaget St., 502/348-4407, 7 A.M.–1 P.M. Tues.–Sat., $0.95–3.95), where treats are turned out fresh each day.

Java Joint (126 N. 3rd St., 502/350-0883, www.thejavajoint.homestead.com, 7:30 A.M.–5:30 P.M. Mon.–Sat., 9:30 A.M.–2:30 P.M. Sun., $5.50–6.75) keeps Bardstown fueled with coffee and specialty drinks all day long, and during the lunch stretch offers a selection of soups, salads, and sandwiches. In addition to the common chicken and egg salad, Java Joint also serves muffalettas, Cubans, and a roasted pepper pimento cheese. On Sunday, a brunch menu offers distinct breakfast and lunch options as well as a potato skin dish that bridges the gap.

American

Hidden away in the basement of Spalding Hall, **◖ Xavier's Restaurant & Lounge** (112 Xavier Dr., 502/349-1116, lunch 11 A.M.–2 P.M. Tues.–Fri., dinner 5–9 P.M. Tues.–Fri., 5–10 P.M. Sat., $7.99–15.99) is worth seeking out. The atmosphere is warm and inviting, and it's one of the best places to go in Bardstown for a special occasion. The menu features steak, seafood, and other favorites, and locals rate the food as some of the tastiest in town.

European

◖ Kreso's Restaurant (218 N. 3rd St., 502/348-5594, www.kresosweb.com, lunch 11 A.M.–3 P.M. Mon.–Fri., dinner 5–11 P.M. Mon.–Fri., 11 A.M.–11 P.M. Sat., noon–10 P.M. Sun., $15–25), which exudes charm thanks to the fact that it is located in an old theater, is the nicest restaurant in Bardstown. Run by a

Bosnian family, the menu offers old-world favorites like schnitzel and goulash, as well as an excellent selection of steaks and seafood (and not the fried kind most popular in these parts). Start any meal with the Bosnian salad, a mix of leaf lettuce, tomato, cucumber, hard-boiled egg, red onion, and feta cheese. The lunch menu ($5.95–10.95) includes lighter versions of popular dinner entrées as well as salads and sandwiches.

Southern

If you want to know what good fried chicken tastes like, get a table at **Kurtz Restaurant** (418 E. Stephen Foster Ave., 502/348-8964, www.bardstownparkview.com, 11 A.M.–9 P.M. Tues.–Sat., noon–8 P.M. Sun., $12.95–18.95), where it's served piping hot and without a hint of grease though it's cooked the way grandma used to do it—in a skillet full of lard. You also don't want to miss the fried cornbread, enormous pieces of meringue pie, or the biscuit pudding with bourbon raisin sauce. Kurtz has been serving fried chicken and other Southern favorites since 1937, and when you step into the home-turned-restaurant you'll be treated like one of the family. The atmosphere is cozy with dining tables spread through the rooms of the house.

Those who like their meals served with a side of history will appreciate the **Old Talbott Tavern** (107 W. Stephen Foster Ave., 502/348-3494, www.talbotts.com, 11 A.M.–8 P.M. Mon.–Fri., 11 A.M.–9 P.M. Sat., 10 A.M.–2 P.M. Sun.), which dates back to 1779 and maintains much of its original architecture. George Rogers Clark used the Tavern as his base during the Revolutionary War, and other famous figures who have passed through the doors include Andrew Jackson, Abraham Lincoln, John James Audubon, and General George Patton. Though portions of fried chicken, catfish, pork chops, and country ham are large, flavors need to be kicked up a notch. Unlike the atmosphere, the food is rather bland.

INFORMATION AND SERVICES

Gather all the information you can handle at Bardstown's **Welcome Center** (1 Court Sq., 502/348-4877, www.visitbardstown.com), located in the courthouse building smack in the middle of the main traffic circle. Bardstown's main **post office** (205 W. Stephen Foster Ave.) is located just down the street.

GETTING THERE

Bardstown is about 40 miles south of Louisville. Take I-65 South to KY 245 South (Exit 112). After 15 miles, turn right on 3rd Street, which leads straight to the center of town. For a more scenic drive, take U.S. 31E (Bardstown Road) all the way from Louisville to Bardstown.

From either Frankfort or Lexington, the trip east to Bardstown takes about one hour on the Martha Layne Collins Blue Grass Parkway.

GETTING AROUND
Trolley Tours

See Bardstown from the windows of the **Heaven Hill Distilleries Trolley** (www.bourbonheritagecenter.com) on a narrated one-hour tour. The handsome, vintage trolley stops at the distillery for a tasting and a peek at the museum and also circles past the town's main attractions. Inquire about times, which change seasonally, at the Welcome Center (1 Court Sq., 502/348-4877, www.visitbardstown.com), where you can also buy tickets ($5). The trolley stop is located on Court Square in front of Old Talbott Tavern.

Carriage Tours

Take in historic Bardstown at a relaxed paced with **Around the Town Carriage Rides** (223 N. 3rd St., 502/249-0889, 9 A.M.–10 P.M. daily). Horse-drawn carriages, buggies, and stagecoaches provide the most stylish rides in town. A 30-minute narrated tour for two people costs $40.

Vicinity of Bardstown

A few small towns surround Bardstown to the south and east, and are worth a visit for their religious and historical sites. Railway enthusiasts and those moved by the writings of Thomas Merton will want to add New Haven to their itinerary, while Lincoln fans can't miss Hodgenville, the president's hometown, and Springfield, his ancestral home.

NEW HAVEN
Abbey of Gethsemani
Since 1848, Trappist monks have called the Abbey of Gethsemani (3642 Monks Rd., Trappist, 502/549-3117, www.monks.org) home, dedicating the time they spend at this beautiful sanctuary to formal prayers and the manual labor that provides their livelihood. Gethsemani is widely known thanks to Thomas Merton, a Trappist monk at the Abbey who wrote multiple books, including his famous autobiography *The Seven Storey Mountain,* and attracted admirers with his interest in interfaith understanding. Visitors to the Abbey are greeted in the Welcome Center with a video that explains the monastic life. Visitors are also invited to join the monks at prayers or Mass. In the longstanding tradition of monks offering hospitality, people interested in prayer and reflection are welcome to reserve a stay at the Abbey (502/549-4133, by donation). Directed retreats are also available through the Merton Institute Retreat Center at Bethany Spring (800/886-7275, www.bethanyspring.org). Visitors to the Abbey of Gethsemani should remember that it is a place of silent prayer.

Kentucky Railway Museum
Chug back in time with a visit to the Kentucky Railway Museum (240 N. Main St., New Haven, 502/549-5470, www.kyrail.org, 10 A.M.–4 P.M. Tues.–Sat., noon–5 P.M. Sun., $5 adults, $2 youth 2–12) and a ride on one of their trains. The trains cover 22 miles of countryside on a 90-minute ride, with a brief layover

at the turn-around point allowing a chance to grab a snack or drink. On select weekends, the only active steam engine in Kentucky steps in for the usual diesel engine, and on every outing, those who have dreamed of engineering a train can opt to ride in the locomotive ($50 adults, $25 youth 7–12). Special events are held throughout the year. Among the most popular are the Great Train Robbery weekends, Mystery Theatre nights, and holiday-themed trips. If you have kids, you won't want to miss Thomas the Tank Engine's visit, which occurs each summer and draws huge crowds. Train rides are offered at 2 P.M. on Saturday and Sunday April–May and November–mid-December; at 11 A.M. and 2 P.M. on Saturday, 2 P.M. on Sunday, and 1 P.M. on Tuesday and Friday mid-June–mid-August; and at 11 A.M. and 2 P.M. on Saturday and 2 P.M. on Sunday mid-August–October. Train fares ($15.50 adults, $10.50 youth 2–12 on diesel trains; $2 more on steam trains) include admission to the museum, which features rail artifacts, and the model train center, which hosts detailed displays that can be activated by visitors.

Getting There and Around
New Haven is located 13.5 miles south of Bardstown and can be reached via southbound U.S. 31E. To reach the Abbey of Gethsemani, you don't have to travel all the way into New Haven. Instead, after eight miles on U.S. 31E, turn left onto Monks Road.

HODGENVILLE
Though Illinois claims to be the Land of Lincoln, America's 16th, and perhaps most popular, president was a Kentuckian by birth and spent the first seven years of his life in the Bluegrass State. More specifically, young Abe grew up in the area that came to be known as Hodgenville but was at the time a frontier town. The early years of his life, a time of struggle though his family would have been considered middle class, certainly helped

shape the man who would become president. In fact, in an autobiography he wrote for his 1860 campaign, Lincoln noted that his earliest memories revolve around his boyhood home on Knobs Creek. Today's Hodgenville celebrates this connection with a number of Lincoln-related sites.

Abraham Lincoln Birthplace and Boyhood Home

Part of the National Park Service, the Abraham Lincoln Birthplace (2995 Lincoln Farm Rd., 270/358-3137, www.nps.gov/abli, 8 A.M.– 4:45 P.M. daily, free admission) and Boyhood Home (seven miles north on U.S. 31E) preserve a sense of how the Lincoln family lived in Kentucky. Begin your visit at the Birthplace Visitors Center, where you can view a 15-minute film about Lincoln's childhood and check out the Lincoln family bible and other artifacts. The site's main attraction is the Memorial Building, a marble and granite structure that houses a cabin symbolic of that in which Lincoln was born. Fifty-six steps, one for each

year of Lincoln's life, lead up to the memorial and past the Sinking Spring, for which the family farm was named. (The Pathway of a President trail provides wheelchair access to the memorial.) A 0.7-mile interpretive hiking trail is open to those who want to stretch their legs and learn a bit about what the Lincoln homestead would have been like. After visiting the Birthplace, continue on to Lincoln's Boyhood Home, where he lived from 1811 to 1816. Poke your head in the family cabin of Lincoln's friend Austin Gollaher, wander down to the creek where Lincoln almost drowned in a flash flood, and examine a garden planted with crops the Lincolns likely grew.

Lincoln Museum

At the Lincoln Museum (66 Lincoln Square, 270/358-3163, www.lincolnmuseum-ky. org, 8:30 A.M.–4:30 P.M. Mon.–Sat., 12:30– 4:30 P.M. Sun., $3 adults, $2.50 seniors, $1.50 youth 5–12), 12 life-size dioramas depict important events in the life of the 16th president—from his cabin years in Kentucky to his

BARDSTOWN

© THERESA DOWELL BLACKINTON

boyhood home of Abraham Lincoln

assassination at Ford's Theatre. The well-done dioramas make history accessible to children and those with only a cursory interest in the subject, while accompanying photos, newspaper articles, letters, and descriptive panels cater to those seeking more in-depth information. A second floor contains Lincoln artwork as well as Civil War artifacts, including items unearthed from battlefield digs.

Lincoln Square Statues

In the center of Hodgenville, two statues of Abraham Lincoln sit facing each other. Dedicated in 1909, Adolph Weinman's Abraham Lincoln Statue depicts the Kentuckian seated and looking as he did when he was president. Directly across from this classic statue you'll find the more whimsical Boy Lincoln Statue, added to the square in 2008. This statue shows young Abe, accompanied by a dog and a fishing pole, leaning against a tree stump and reading from a Webster's spelling book.

Entertainment

For a toe-tapping good time that apparently even the President would have loved, make plans to attend the **Lincoln Jamboree** (2579 Lincoln Farm Rd., 270/358-3545, www.lincolnjamboree.com, 7:30–10:30 P.M. Sat., $8.50), an old-fashioned country music show that's been going strong for over 50 years. Come early to enjoy Southern gospel music on the patio (6 P.M.).

Events

To honor the city's, as well as the state's, greatest resident, Hodgenville celebrates **Lincoln Days** (270/358-8710, www.lincolndays.org) annually in late September or early October. The weekend festival includes an oratory contest, Mary Todd and Abraham Lincoln look-alike contests, and pioneer games, as well as art and car shows, a parade, a fun run, and live music.

Accommodations

Though most people visit Hodgenville on a day trip, those with a passion for history and unusual accommodations will want to spend the night at **Nancy Lincoln Inn** (2975 Lincoln Farm Rd., 270/358-3845, $69). Located immediately adjacent to Lincoln's Birthplace, with uninterrupted views of the Memorial, the Inn is made up of four cabins, each built in 1929 from chestnut logs and featuring restored pine floors and double beds. Though the cabins have electricity and air-conditioning, you won't find TVs distracting you from the surrounding nature and history, and toilets and showers are located in a shared bathhouse. Owner Carl Howell Jr. knows just about everything about Lincoln, and he's happy to answer questions or talk history.

Food

Laha's Red Castle (21 Lincoln Square, 270/358-9201, 9 A.M.–4 P.M. Mon.–Tues. and Thurs.–Sat., 9 A.M.–1:30 P.M. Wed., $1.95–4.95) has been keeping Hodgenville in hamburgers for over 65 years. Follow the smell of fried onions to the tiny corner diner, where you'll most likely have to wait for a stool at the counter to open up before you can place your order for a fresh-made hamburger and an ice cold Coke.

Follow up your lunch with a treat from **The Sweet Shoppe** (100 S. Lincoln Blvd., 270/358-0424, www.sweetshoppefudge.com, 11 A.M.–6 P.M. Mon.–Sat.), which offers 35 flavors of fudge, along with ice cream and other desserts. A half-pound of fudge sells for $4.99.

Information and Services

The **LaRue County Visitors Center** (60 Lincoln Sq., 270/358-3411, www.laruecountychamber.org, 9 A.M.–4 P.M. Mon.–Fri.) can set you up with all the information you need on Hodgenville attractions as well as other regional sites of interest.

Getting There

Hodgenville is located 25 miles southwest of Bardstown and can be reached in 30 minutes by following southbound U.S. 31E. Hodgenville can also be reached by exiting

I-65 at southbound KY 61 (Exit 91), which will lead you right to the center of town.

SPRINGFIELD

Complementing Hodgenville is the town of Springfield, which is where President Lincoln's pioneer grandparents settled and where both of his parents were born and raised.

Lincoln Homestead State Park

Abraham Lincoln's ancestors entered Kentucky in the late 1700s via the Wilderness Road, establishing a homestead in the area that is now Springfield. Lincoln Homestead State Park (5079 Lincoln Park Rd., 859/336-7461, http://parks.ky.gov) is home to three structures that preserve the history of the Lincoln family. The Lincoln Cabin is a replica of the log house in which Abraham Lincoln's grandmother lived and raised five children, including President Lincoln's father Thomas. A second log house at the park, which is a bit fancier with a second floor and glass windows, was the home of President Lincoln's mother Nancy Hanks. This original cabin was moved to the park from about a mile away. A third building, a stately white home that belonged to President Lincoln's favorite uncle Mordecai Lincoln, is also in the park, having been moved from across the street. Tours of the cabins along with a blacksmith's shop cost $2 for adults and $1.50 for youth and are offered 10:30 A.M.–5:30 P.M. daily May–September and on weekends in October. The grounds, which are complete with signage relaying the history of the buildings and area, are free and open year-round.

Opposite the road from the homes is an 18-hole golf course, allowing you to play a round on the rolling hills where the Lincolns once lived.

Mt. Zion Covered Bridge

At 246 feet long, the Mt. Zion Covered Bridge (KY 458), which crosses the Beech Fork River, is one of the longest remaining multi-span bridges in Kentucky. Built in 1871, Mt. Zion Covered Bridge is the only one of Washington County's seven covered bridges to remain standing, though it is no longer in use. On your way to see the bridge, be sure to make a detour at **Valley Hill Store** (65 Valley Hill Rd., 859/336-0266, 1–7 P.M. Wed. and Sun., 10 A.M.–7 P.M. Thurs.–Sat.), a store opened in 1896 in what was then the L&N depot.

Accommodations

◖ **Maple Hill Manor** (2941 Perryville Rd., Springfield, 859/336-3075, www.maplehill-manor.com, $129–179) deserves the many raves and honors it has received. Set on a 15-acre working alpaca and llama farm and surrounded by horse, tobacco, and cattle farms, this wonderfully preserved antebellum home has seven lovely guestrooms, each with private bath. The large, light-filled rooms are luxurious with plush bedding, towels, and robes, high-end bath products, fireplaces, TVs, and Internet access. Homemade desserts and beverages are offered each evening in the parlor, and a candlelight breakfast is served on fine china in the formal dining room each morning. Guests are invited to tour the grounds, which are complete with flower gardens, fish ponds, and an orchard from which you can pick fresh fruit in season. Though convenient to Springfield attractions and the Bourbon Trail, Maple Hill Manor is also the perfect place to go and do nothing but relax. Football fans take note: Maple Hill Manor was the childhood home of Super Bowl MVP and Giants quarterback Phil Simms.

Food

Signature dishes at **Mordecai's on Main** (105 W. Main St., 859/336-3500, www.mordecaisonmain.com, 11 A.M.–midnight Tues.–Sat., 10 A.M.–2 P.M. Sun., $6.49–18.49) include honey bourbon salmon, chicken in a mushroom bourbon cream sauce, New York strip marinated in bourbon, and bourbon-marinated pork chops, making it a perfect place for Bourbon Trail visitors to dine. If you've already had enough bourbon, the menu also offers burgers, sandwiches, and entrées prepared in other tasty ways. Located in a downtown building, Mordecai's is decorated with historic photos and offers a variety of seating options, including patio seating in the summer. Good food and good service make this Springfield's best dining option. The Friday and Saturday buffet is extremely popular, offering a selection of entrées as well as soup and salad.

Information and Services

The **Springfield Tourism Commission** (127 W. Main St., 859/336-5440, www.seespringfieldky.com, 9 A.M.–5 P.M. Mon.–Fri.) has an office in the restored Opera House. After you gather any information you need, take a few minutes for an informal tour of the building, which was built around 1900 and renovated in 2004.

Getting There and Around

Springfield is 17 miles east of Bardstown on U.S. 150. Located right past the intersection of U.S. 150 and KY 55, Springfield is on the route between Bardstown and Lebanon and thus easy to add to any Bourbon Trail itinerary.

The Bourbon Trail and Nearby Towns

In 1999, the Kentucky Distillers Association decided to turn one of the state's most distinct industries into what is now one of its biggest tourist attractions, creating an official Bourbon Trail that linked six major distilleries located in the heart of central Kentucky. To travel that trail is to get a taste of Kentucky, both literally and figuratively, as it encompasses not only bourbon distilleries but also small towns and rolling countryside. The official trail isn't, however, a comprehensive tour of the region, which is why this section also includes nearby towns, where key components of bourbon distillation are made and where small-town Kentucky life is perfectly lived day in and day out. For bourbon aficionados as well as those new to the drink, a Bourbon Trail road trip is a must.

CLERMONT

For those driving the trail from west to east, Clermont is the starting point. Clermont, however, is not actually a city or even a town. It's really just a stop on the road with a small number of homes and businesses. Therefore most Bourbon Trail travelers group Clermont with Bardstown and visit it on a brief detour. From Louisville, which is where many people begin their trip, Clermont is directly on the way to Bardstown.

Jim Beam American Outpost

The tours at Jim Beam American Outpost (526 Happy Hollow Rd., 502/543-9877, 9:30 A.M.–3:30 P.M. Mon.–Sat., free) do not include the distillery, but instead cover the grounds and the Beam Home. Visitors are also invited to view a short video about the distilling process and sample some Jim Beam bourbons. For those doing the entire Bourbon Trail or a significant portion of it, the Outpost is worth a visit; however, if you only have time for one distillery, you'll have a more in-depth experience at one of the Trail's other stops.

Bernheim Arboretum

Grateful for his success in the whiskey business, Isaac W. Bernheim chose to give back to the state of Kentucky by purchasing 14,000 acres for use as an arboretum. Designed by the Olmsted landscape firm, Bernheim Arboretum and Research Center (2499 Old State Hwy. 245, 502/955-8512, www.bernheim.org, 7 A.M.–sunset daily, free weekdays, $5 per car weekends and holidays) opened to the public in 1950 and has since become an oasis for people all around the region. Begin your visit at the LEED Platinum Certified Visitors Center, a magnificent "green" building where you can pick up maps, learn about the arboretum, browse the gift shop, or enjoy

THE BOURBON CHASE

While most people choose to cover the Bourbon Trail in an automobile, some believe the best way to take in the landscape of this part of Kentucky is on foot. Hence, the reason the annual Bourbon Chase (www.bourbonchase. com), a 200-mile relay race along the Bourbon Trail, sells out every year months before its October start date.

Teams of 6 or 12 members begin the race at Jim Beam Distillery in Clermont, with teams taking off every 15 minutes during the first day. Each runner covers between three and eight miles before being replaced by a teammate. The course moves from Clermont to Bardstown, then passes through Loretto,

Lebanon, Springfield, Perryville, Stanford, Danville, Harrodsburg, Lawrenceburg, Versailles, Frankfort, and Midway, before ending in Lexington, where a huge party awaits participants. The race can take up to 36 hours, with runners pounding the pavement both day and night. Towns along the way are set up to support and celebrate the teams regardless of what hour the runners and their teammates pass through.

Autumn is a beautiful time of year to visit the Bourbon Trail region of Kentucky, so whether you're interested in participating in the race or just cheering on the runners, put the Bourbon Chase on your calendar.

BARDSTOWN

a snack or light lunch at the café. The arboretum offers plenty of activities. Those seeking more passive recreation opportunities can picnic, view wildlife, and wander around the arboretums many gardens and collections, including an open prairie habitat and the largest holly collection in North America. If you're after something more active, take advantage of the arboretum's 35 miles of hiking trails, 3.7-mile bike trail, roadside bike lanes, and the fishing areas at Lake Nevin. Be sure to check out the Canopy Tree Walk, a boardwalk that puts you 75 feet over the forest floor and offers splendid views year-round, though autumn is especially breathtaking. Hikers will find the 13.75-mile Millennium Trail through the knobs of Kentucky to be one of the region's best trails. Bernheim offers a robust schedule of events that includes moonlight hikes, ECO Kids activities, art classes, and seasonal festivities. Check their website for a full listing.

Accommodations and Food

Just north of Bernheim and Jim Beam, you'll find a strip of fast food restaurants as well as a chain hotel or two. There's no real reason to stay overnight in the area, and with Clermont located in between Bardstown and Louisville, you have plenty of options in either direction. Your best bet for lunch is to bring a picnic and enjoy it on the grounds of Bernheim or check out the tasty sandwiches at their café.

Getting There

Clermont is about 15 miles northwest of Bardstown. From the center of Bardstown, take Third Street to northbound KY 245, where you'll turn left and then travel about 13.5 miles to reach Clermont's attractions.

Clermont is about 27 miles south of downtown Louisville. To get to Clermont, simply follow southbound I-65 to the KY 245 exit (Exit 112). Turn left onto KY 245, and you'll find Bernheim on your right and Jim Beam just past it on your left.

LORETTO

The next stop on your west-to-east tour of Kentucky's bourbon distilleries, after you check out the distilleries in Clermont and Bardstown, is Loretto. Best described as a hamlet, Loretto, with a population of about 600, probably wouldn't make the map if it weren't for the iconic Maker's Mark distillery being located here.

◖ Maker's Mark Distillery

Set on a village-like campus, Maker's Mark Distillery (3350 Burks Spring Rd., 270/865-2099, www.makersmark.com, free tours) wins the award for most picturesque distillery. The buildings are uniformly dark brown, tan, and red—the trademark colors of Maker's Mark—with cut-out bourbon bottles on every window shutter. The tour starts in a home museum decorated to the 1950 period when the Samuels family began Maker's Mark. It then takes in the spotless distillery, where bourbon is still brewed in wooden vats; the bottling line, where the bottles are dipped in their famous red wax; and the warehouse, where barrels are still rotated during their six-year aging process. The finale is a well-conducted tasting of the distillery's signature bourbon. Tours are offered once an hour on the half-hour 10:30 A.M.–3:30 P.M. Monday–Saturday year-round. Sunday tours are offered March–December at 1:30 P.M., 2:30 P.M., and 3:30 P.M.

Sisters of Loretto

Founded on the Kentucky frontier in 1812, the Sisters of Loretto (515 Nerinx Rd., 270/865-2621, www.lorettocommunity.org) moved to their current campus in 1824. Visitors are welcome on the campus, a place of mesmerizing beauty that in addition to preserving vast wild spaces also supports a working farm and many historical buildings. Don't miss the Rhodes Hall Art Gallery, where the amazing sculptures of Sister Jeanne Dueber are displayed. You'll also want to stroll the walking paths and visit the cemetery and AIDS garden. The Sisters of Loretto welcome retreatants. Those seeking solitude and reflection should inquire about staying in one of the seven Cedars of Peace cabins on campus.

Accommodations and Food

Although **Hill House Bed and Breakfast** (110 Holy Cross Rd., 270/865-2300, www.thehillhouseky.com, $105–130) dates to the 1800s, the house has been completely gutted and renovated. Save for the original floors and staircase, Hill House is basically a brand new house

and thus sports completely modern rooms and amenities, though antique furniture and classic stylings make the four queen guest rooms as well as the common areas feel warm and inviting. Guests are not only treated to a delicious breakfast but are also offered wine and cheese in the afternoon.

Loretto is a very small community. For additional accommodation options, as well as a selection of restaurants, head to Lebanon, which is just a few miles southeast.

Getting There

From Bardstown, you can take southbound KY 49 all the way to Loretto, but be warned that it's a windy road, and the 17-mile distance between the towns will feel much longer. Another option is to drive 16 miles on eastbound U.S. 150 toward Springfield to southbound KY 55, and then continue 9 miles to Lebanon. From there, it's 10 miles up northbound KY 49 to Loretto.

LEBANON

Lebanon likes to call itself the heart of Kentucky, because it is located at the state's geographic center. As a good-time partying town, it's also got quite a lively pulse. If you're looking for a town on the Bourbon Trail where you can enjoy a drink after the distillery tour is over, you've found your spot. Named for the biblical Lebanon that is supposed to be part of the Promised Land, Lebanon, Kentucky, is the gateway to Maker's Mark, and a good mid-way stopping point as you travel the Bourbon Trail.

Kentucky Cooperage

One visit to a distillery and you'll know how important the barrels are to bourbon making. It wouldn't be bourbon without them. Therefore to get a full understanding of bourbon, you need to head to Kentucky Cooperage (712 E. Main St., 270/692-4674, www.independentstavecompany.com, tours at 9:30 A.M. and 1 P.M. Mon.–Fri., free), where most of Kentucky's bourbon barrels are made. The tour has three stops—one in the stave, where

BARDSTOWN

PENN'S STORE

Located in the blink-and-you-miss-it hamlet of Gravel Switch, Penn's Store (www.pennsstore.com, 859/332-7706) is the oldest country store in the United States continuously run by the same family. Since 1850 the Penn family has been behind the counter at this historic landmark, selling the local community groceries, sandwiches, dried herbs, and other essentials. These days, plenty of tourists find their way to the store, which looks about the same now as it did when it opened. Go ahead and browse the aisles, take photos, and buy a t-shirt, but don't forget to take some time to chat with Jeanne Penn Lane, the current owner of the store and the holder of a wealth of knowledge and more than a few good stories.

On Sunday afternoons, musicians and singers gather for pickin' and singin' on the front porch. Penn's Store's biggest event, however, is the Great Outhouse Blowout, held every October. The classic car show and live entertainment is excellent, but what people really come to see are the racing outhouses. The event began in 1992 as a way to dedicate the first and only restroom Penn's Store has ever had. It's an honest-to-God outhouse, and you're welcome to use it if you've got to go.

Penn's Store is open 11 A.M.-5 P.M. Saturday and 2-5 P.M. Sunday April-November, 11 A.M.-4 P.M. Saturday and 1-4 P.M. Sunday December-March. If you're in the area on a weekday, call and inquire as to whether the store is open. Ms. Lane will often throw open the doors if she knows you're coming by.

There's no actual address for Penn's Store but it's not too difficult to find. From Lebanon, drive east on U.S. 68 for 10.5 miles. Then turn right onto KY 243, which you'll remain on through Gravel Switch and as it turns left at an intersection with KY 337. After a couple of miles, KY 243 will turn right. Stay on KY 243, cross a bridge, and then immediately turn right on the road leading directly to the store.

© THERESA DOWELL BLACKINTON

the privy at Penn's Store

barrels are constructed; one in the finishing room, where the all-important charring is done; and one at the cooper's, where barrels that don't pass inspection are repaired by hand. Informative videos are shown at each stop, filling you in on any processes that you might not see firsthand. Because this is a factory tour, closed toe shoes are required.

Lebanon National Cemetery

Designated a national cemetery in 1867, the land that became Lebanon National Cemetery (20 KY 208, 270/692-3390, sunrise–sunset daily) was first used to bury 865 Union dead from the 1862 Battle of Perryville. Since then, service members from all of the United States's wars have been, and continue to be, interred here. Take a stroll on the somber grounds to remember the sacrifices made by soldiers standing in defense of the United States. Services take place on Memorial and Veterans Day, and the cemetery participates in the Wreaths Across America program in December.

BARDSTOWN

© THERESA DOWELL BLACKINTON

Lebanon National Cemetery

Agritourism

Lebanon is surrounded by agricultural land, with farmers growing crops and raising livestock on acres of rich land. Many of these farms welcome visits by the public, though because they are all working farms, they do ask that visitors make arrangements in advance.

Alpacas have become a popular farm animal in recent years, and at **Serenity Farm** (1380 Frogg Lane, Raywick, 270/692-8743) owner Tim Auch will gladly show you around and introduce you to his animals. More common to Kentucky are horses, which you can find at **Meadow Creek Farm** (KY 49 & KY 84, 270/692-0021). Though Kentucky is best known for its thoroughbred horses, the area around Lebanon is standardbred territory, and Meadow Creek produces the best standardbreds around, including world champion Sportswriter.

One of many such displays in the state, the **Marion County Quilt Trail** takes visitors on a tour of the countryside in search of 45 quilt patches decorating barns and other structures.

Pick up a brochure at the Lebanon visitors center (239 N. Spalding Ave., Ste. 200, 270/692-0021, www.visitlebanonky.com, 8 A.M.–5 P.M. Mon.–Fri.) for more information on each of the designs as well as suggestions for other sites to look for along the way. You'll even learn how to identify different breeds of cow.

Tours

Because Lebanon was home to a train depot and Union Commissary, it felt the wrath of Confederate General John Hunt Morgan on all three of his Civil War raids into Kentucky. A self-guided walking or driving tour points out sites of interest located along the **John Hunt Morgan Trail.** After completing this tour, head to nearby Bradfordsville to explore the **William Clark Quantrill Trail,** a route that commemorates sites related to the notorious outlaw's guerilla attacks.

Architecture buffs may prefer the **Historic Homes & Landmarks Tour,** which offers separate walking and driving tours and points out buildings of note, many of which date to before the Civil War. Brochures with maps for all tours are available at the visitors center.

Nightlife

As someone explained it to me: Some places in Kentucky are dry; some are wet; and some, like Lebanon, are soaking wet. Once a famous party town thanks to the former Club 68—which hosted the likes of Tina Turner, CCR, and Little Richard—Lebanon is no longer as wild as it once was, but the town still knows how to have a good time. On weekends, set your sights on the Main Street area bars, which are easy to hop between. Popular spots include **The Oak Barrel** (202 W. Main St., Lebanon, 270/692-1295), **Chasers** (110 N. Proctor Knott Ave., 270/699-2221), and **Cardinal Den** (225 W. ML King, 270/692-1125). Closing hours are variable depending on crowds, but you can expect these three bars to stay open until midnight on weeknights and until 2 A.M. or later on weekends.

Festivals and Events

Lebanon complements their nightlife with a packed schedule of festivals, oftentimes putting on two or three events at once. Check the tourism website for a full listing of festivals.

The year's biggest event is **Marion County Country Ham Days** (www.visitlebanonky. com), held on the last weekend of September. In addition to offering all the country ham a person could possibly consume, the festival features the PIGasus parade, a hog calling contest, a car show, carnival, 5K race, and live entertainment.

Fans of radio-controlled planes won't want to miss the week-long **Jets Over Kentucky** (www.visitlebanonky.com), which takes place at the Lebanon–Springfield Airport in early July. Over 100 pilots put their jets to the test in dogfights, aerobatic competitions, and other contests. Spectators are welcome to enjoy the show and chat with pilots.

Beat the winter doldrums by attending the **Kentucky Bluegrass Music Kickoff** (www. visitlebanonky.com), which features play-alongs, workshops, and a Saturday night concert headlined by big names in bluegrass. The kickoff is held on a Friday and Saturday in early January.

Recreation

Two fishing spots are located just outside downtown Lebanon. Both **Fagan Branch Reservoir** (370 Fagan Branch Rd.) and **Marion County Sportsman's Lake** (716 Sportsman Lake Rd.) are stocked with largemouth bass, smallmouth bass, bluegill, and other popular species. At Fagan Branch Reservoir, you'll also find the Cecil L. Gorley Naturalist Trail, a 3.2-mile loop around the lake that has a notable 43 bridges. The grounds at Sportsman's Lake are open for deer, squirrel, and waterfowl hunting, and also contain archery and skeet ranges.

Take in a 100-mile view that encompasses three counties at **Scott's Ridge Lookout** (KY 84). From a maintained perch, you can look out over a wide swath of farmland, the panorama seemingly endless. The view takes on remarkably different characteristics with each season.

Accommodations

Apparently even John Hunt Morgan and his Raiders found the classic home that is now **Myrtledene Bed and Breakfast** (370 N. Spalding Ave., Lebanon, 270/692-2223. www. myrtledene.com, $95) to be beautiful, as they spared it during their raids through the state. In fact, instead of setting it on fire, they turned it into their headquarters while in Lebanon. Reserve one of the four rooms, and enjoy the sense of history preserved in the B&B, which is furnished in antiques. On a nice day take advantage of the grounds, which are complete with fish ponds, hammocks, and swings. Should the weather not cooperate, the rooms are fully equipped with television and wireless Internet, and the house has a library and piano.

Those looking for a standard hotel should book a room at the **Hampton Inn** (1125 Loretto Rd., 270/699-4000, www.hamptoninn.com, $92), which is fresh and clean and provides all the modern amenities. A free all-you-can eat hot breakfast is offered each morning.

The **Rosewood Cabins** (520 Fairway Dr., 270/692-0506, www.rosewoodgolfcourse.com) are an excellent choice for families or groups of friends, with three queen bedrooms and one pull-out couch per cabin. The cabins also have fully equipped kitchens and laundry rooms. Golfers will particularly enjoy these cabins as they are located on a course, and cabin rental allows for unlimited golf. In summertime, access to the clubhouse pool is also included. On weekends, there is a two-night minimum ($159), while cabins are rented by the night Sunday–Thursday ($70).

Food

The Oak Barrel (202 W. Main St., Lebanon, 270/692-1295, lunch 11 A.M.–2 P.M. Mon.–Fri., dinner 4 P.M.–midnight Tues.–Sat., $10–30) serves up a tasty menu of upscale American food. Prices and portion sizes are more in-line with big city restaurants, but quality is also high. The glazed pork and Grand Marnier chicken get good reviews. The attractive oak barrel bar draws a crowd, especially on weekends when drinks are complemented by live music.

The people behind **Ragetti's Fine Italian Dining** (213 W. Main St., 270/692-1322, 11 A.M.–10 P.M. Mon.–Thurs., 11 A.M.–11 P.M. Fri.–Sat., noon–8 P.M. Sun., $5.95–10.95) have transformed a former Hardee's into a cozy restaurant decorated with old photos of Lebanon. You'll find hearty pastas, filling pizzas, and a broad selection of subs and strombolis on the menu. Half-portions are available at lunch, and unless you skipped breakfast, it's more than enough food to take you to dinner.

Fans of home cooking will want to have a meal at **Willie A's** (201 N. Depot St., 270/692-3902, 6–8:30 A.M. and 11 A.M.–2 P.M. Mon.–Fri., $4.95–8.95), where your plate will be filled with traditional favorites like barbecue, potato salad, cornbread, and mashed potatoes. A lovely al fresco dining area now graces the historic building, which once hosted those traveling through Lebanon on the L&N railroad.

If you're looking for a little flavor in your life, consider **La Fuente** (300 W. Main St., 270/692-0722, 11 A.M.–10 P.M. Sun.–Thurs., 11 A.M.–10:30 P.M. Fri.–Sat.). Though you might wonder how good a Mexican restaurant in the heart of Kentucky can be, you'd be wrong not to give it a chance. Thanks to the area's agricultural nature, a significant population of Hispanics call Lebanon home, and the food at La Fuente is made to please even the most discerning palates.

Information and Services

Tucked away on the second floor of the former junior high school, in what is now called Centre Square, the friendly folks at the **Lebanon Tourist & Convention Commission** (239 N. Spalding Ave., Ste. 200, 270/692-0021, www.visitlebanonky.com, 8 A.M.–5 P.M. Mon.–Fri.) will gladly help you plan your visit to Lebanon. Heck, they might even volunteer to show your around themselves, so be sure to stop in and load up on insider tips.

Getting There and Around

From Bardstown, take eastbound U.S. 150 about 16 miles to southbound KY 55, which will, after an additional nine miles, land you on Lebanon's Main Street. If you're coming from Frankfort or Lexington, take westbound Martha Layne Collins Blue Grass Parkway to southbound KY 555 (Exit 42). After about 15 miles, KY 555 becomes KY 55; continue straight for another 9 miles to reach Lebanon. From either city, the trip should take about one hour and 15 minutes.

Lebanon is located along U.S. 68, which is designated a scenic highway in Kentucky. It begins in Western Kentucky near Illinois, and then travels east and northeast, passing through Land Between the Lakes, Bowling Green, Lexington, and many smaller towns in between before exiting into Ohio at Maysville. If you're looking for a scenic driving route, U.S. 68 is a good one. Locally, you can take it to reach Perryville and Harrodsburg in the Lexington and Horse Country region of the state.

When driving around the area, be particularly watchful for deer as they are abundant in the area and dangerous to motorists. If you see one cross the road, proceed with extreme caution since others are usually nearby.

LAWRENCEBURG

Lawrenceburg specializes in the fine things in life, which here in Kentucky are bourbon, wine, and cigars made with Kentucky tobacco. Visitors are invited to tour sites related to all three, and no one's going to stop you from taking as many souvenirs of each with you as you'd like. Within easy reach of Frankfort, Lawrenceburg is a small town with a quaint downtown surrounded by farmland.

Four Roses Distillery

Because its bourbons were sold only as exports until 2003, Four Roses Distillery (1224 Bonds Mill Rd., 502/839-3436, www.fourroses.us, tours on the hour 9 A.M.–3 P.M. Mon.–Sat., free) is not as well known as other Kentucky distilleries. It does, however, offer tours of its production facilities as well as tastings. The tours last about 45 minutes, shorter than most and thus perfect for those on a tight schedule. Four Roses also has the most notable

architecture of the state's distilleries, with its facilities housed inside a Spanish Mission–style building.

Wild Turkey Distillery

The tour at Wild Turkey Distillery (1525 Tyrone Rd., 502/839-2182, www.wildturkeybourbon.com, tours at 9 A.M., 10:30 A.M., 12:30 P.M., and 2:30 P.M. Mon.–Sat., free) provides one of the most in-depth looks at the process by which raw grains are turned into smooth bourbon. After watching a short film featuring master distiller Jimmy Russell, who has been at Wild Turkey for over 55 years, visitors witness production step-by-step. Watch a grain truck empty its load, see the yeast starter and grain mash being pumped into the fermenter, poke your head into vats in various stages of fermentation, compare the bourbon-to-be after the first and the second condensation and distillation, and observe the filling of barrels. Should you find yourself a little bit thirsty at the end of the tour, hang around for a free sampling of the products.

© THERESA DOWELL BLACKINTON

vineyards at Lovers Leap in early spring

BARDSTOWN

Lovers Leap Vineyards & Winery

With 30 acres of vines set on a total of 66 acres, Lovers Leap Vineyards & Winery (1180 Lanes Mill Rd., 502/839-1299, www. loversleapwine.com, 11 A.M.–5 P.M. Mon.–Thurs., 11 A.M.–8 P.M. Fri.–Sat., 1–5 P.M. Sun.) is the largest vineyard in Kentucky, producing 10 percent of the state's grape crop. The Leet Family, who bought the vineyard in 2008 and do every step from growing the grapes to bottling the final product on-site, produce white, blush, red, and dessert wines that have medaled at competitions in California, New York, Texas, and Kentucky. One of their more unique (and tasty) offerings is a red wine composed of seven different varietals and humorously named Sloppy Seconds. Whether you're a wine connoisseur or you don't know your chardonnay from your shiraz, you'll be warmly welcomed to the vineyard and invited to indulge in a tasting (6 wines for $5) or participate in a tour of the vineyard. Summer evenings feature live music, and events often occur on weekends. Future plans include adding a café and B&B to the property.

Kentucky Gentlemen Cigars

At Kentucky Gentlemen Cigars (1056 Ninevah Rd., 502/839-9226, www.kentuckygentlemencigars.com), two of Kentucky's most heralded products—bourbon and tobacco—are combined to make cigars that have gotten the attention of cigar fans around the nation and world. To make the hand-rolled cigars, tobacco is aged for six months in used bourbon barrels. Though the bourbon cigars are most popular, Kentucky Gentlemen Cigars also produces moonshine, mint julep, wine, and other flavored cigars. Stop by to see the production process and learn about this Kentucky Proud business.

Events

Exalting burgoo, a spicy barbecue-style stew popular in Kentucky, the **Anderson County Burgoo Festival** (www.kentuckyburgoo.com) is held annually in Lawrenceburg on the last weekend of September. The main point of the festival is to sample as much burgoo as you can handle, but for a little balance, live music, art and history exhibitions, pageants, and tractor pulls are also on the schedule.

Food

Heavens to Betsy (124 Main St., 502/859-9291, 6 A.M.–6 P.M. Mon.–Fri., 7 A.M.–4 P.M. Sat., $5.95–7.95) specializes in bakery items and sandwiches. Grab a homemade muffin for breakfast. For lunch, take your pick of deli sandwiches with a side of pasta, potato, three-bean, or apple-pineapple salad. Cake, of course, is delicious any time of day.

Café on Main (116 Main St., 502/839-8390, www.cafeonmainky.food.officelive.com, 10:30 A.M.–8 P.M. Tues.–Thurs., 10:30 A.M.–9 P.M. Fri.–Sat., 10:30 A.M.–2 P.M. Sun., $5.95–16.95) offers a selection of sandwiches named for Kentucky Derby winners for lunch, while the dinner menu features entrées that range from fried frog legs to prime rib. Late breakfast is also available.

Information and Services

The **Anderson County Tourism Commission** (502/517-6362, www.visitlawrenceburg-andersonco.com) can provide you with information on Lawrenceburg. While in town, stop in City Hall (100 N. Main St., 9 A.M.–5 P.M. Mon.–Fri.), where tourist information is available in the foyer of the historic building.

Getting There and Around

Lawrenceburg lies at the intersection of U.S. 62 and U.S. 127. It's about 15 miles south of Frankfort on U.S. 127, and about 24 miles west of Lexington if you take U.S. 60 to Versailles and then switch to U.S. 62. From Bardstown, travel 34 miles on eastbound Martha Layne Collins Blue Grass Parkway to northbound U.S. 127, which after five miles will lead to Lawrenceburg. If you're coming from nearby Danville or Harrodsburg, just follow northbound U.S. 127.

Frankfort

A favorite Kentucky joke asks "How do you pronounce the capital of Kentucky: Loo-IS-ville or Loo-EE-ville?" And while neither of those is the correct way to pronounce Louisville, the joke is that no matter how you pronounce it, Louisville is not the capital of Kentucky. Small, unassuming Frankfort is actually the capital of the Bluegrass State. Unlike the majority of state capitals, Frankfort is neither big nor bustling. Sure, when government is in session, there's a bit more traffic on the roads and in the restaurants, but life still goes on at a measured pace and remains overwhelmingly hassle free. Though politics can be ugly, Frankfort is charming. Attractive historic buildings line downtown streets, through which trains still pass daily; a "singing" bridge helps traffic move across the Kentucky River, which flows right through the city; and a plethora of parks preserve tracts of lush land perfect for picnicking, hiking, biking, and wildlife-watching.

GOVERNMENT SIGHTS
Kentucky State Capitol

The Kentucky State Capitol (700 Capital Ave., 502/564-3449, www.historicproperties.ky.gov, 8 A.M.–4:30 P.M. Mon.–Fri., free), a beaux arts building with classical French influences throughout, celebrated its centennial in 2010. Visitors to the capitol will first notice the statues in the first-floor rotunda, which represent important figures in Kentucky history: President Abraham Lincoln, Statesman Henry Clay, Dr. Ephraim McDowell, Vice President Alben Barkley, and President of the Confederacy Jefferson Davis. Each level of the government occupies a floor of the capitol: the executive branch is located on the first floor, the judicial branch on the second, and the legislative branch on the third. In addition to visiting the House and Senate chambers and the Supreme Court, don't miss the State Reception Room on the second floor, which puts one in

© THERESA DOWELL BLACKINTON

Kentucky State Capitol

BARDSTOWN

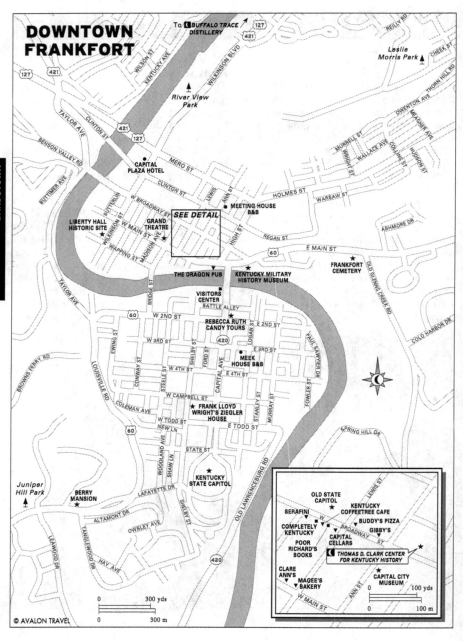

© AVALON TRAVEL

mind of the Palace of Versailles thanks to its mirrors and chandeliers as well as its intricate decor. Visitors can ask for a map at the tour desk and explore the capitol on their own or inquire about guided tours being offered that day. An ID is required for admission.

The grounds of the capitol are notable in their own right, designed by the Olmsted brothers, sons of legendary landscape architect Frederick Law Olmsted. The **Capitol Grounds Walking Tour** brochure, available at the desk inside the capitol or on the capitol website, outlines a route with stops at 37 sites. One of these stops is at the **Floral Clock,** which measures 34 feet across and is filled seasonally with over 10,000 plants.

The Executive Mansion, home to the governor and his family, is also located in the capitol complex. The mansion, built in the same beaux arts style as the capitol and specifically fashioned after one of Marie Antoinette's villas, is one of only a handful of executive residences open to the public. Free tours are offered 9–11 A.M. on Tuesday and Thursday, but require an appointment (502/564-3449) and may be canceled if an event is being held at the mansion.

MUSEUMS AND HISTORICAL SIGHTS
◖ Thomas D. Clark Center for Kentucky History

As the one and only museum dedicated to Kentucky history—12,000 years of it— the Thomas D. Clark Center for Kentucky History (100 W. Broadway, 502/564-1792, http://history.ky.gov, 10 A.M.–4 P.M. Wed., 10 A.M.–8 P.M. Thurs., 10 A.M.–5 P.M. Fri.– Sat., $4 adults, $2 youth 6–18) is home to a rich collection of artifacts, a portion of which are displayed in the center's permanent exhibit, with others appearing in temporary exhibits. The permanent exhibit, A Kentucky Journey, tells the story of the state era by era with the help of authentic items as well as hands-on activities and animatronic characters. Don't miss Museum Theater, an impressive performance series in which on-staff actors write and present short plays about various aspects of Kentucky history. Performances take place on Saturday afternoons at 1 P.M. and 3 P.M. as well as at varying times during the week. Check the online calendar for the current schedule. Admission to the Center also includes admission to the Old State Capitol.

Genealogists will want to visit the center's **Martin F. Schmidt Library,** which is the premiere center for Kentucky genealogy research. Family history workshops held on the second Saturday of every month help those interested in tracing their roots establish a plan and identify resources.

Old State Capitol

Because the plans for the current state capitol required more space than was available at the site of the third capitol (the first two burnt down), the Old State Capitol (Broadway and St. Clair St., 502/564-1792, http://history. ky.gov, 10 A.M.–4 P.M. Wed., 10 A.M.–8 P.M. Thurs., 10 A.M.–5 P.M. Fri.–Sat., $4 adults, $2 youth 6–18) was not demolished when the new capitol was opened in 1910, and to this day still stands as a monument to history. Designed by Gideon Shyrock and meant to resemble a Greek temple, the Old State Capitol was built out of Kentucky marble (aka limestone) and was considered architecturally advanced when completed in 1830. The circular staircase, held in place by a single keystone, is indeed remarkable and a must-see for architecture buffs. Tours take you into the House and Senate chambers, furnished mainly in reproduction furniture but with original paintings; the library; the court chambers; and the first floor office rooms, which house an exhibit on the capitol lawn—host to everything from cattle to concerts. Admission to the Old State Capitol also includes admission to the Thomas D. Clark Center for Kentucky History.

Kentucky Military History Museum

The Old State Arsenal is being repurposed to house the Kentucky Military History Museum

(125 E. Main St., 502/564-1792, http://history.ky.gov), which, along with the Center for Kentucky History and the Old State Capitol, is under the ownership of the Kentucky Historical Society. At the time of research, the museum was open on Saturdays only for tours that primarily focus on the architecture of the building (10 A.M.–5 P.M., reserve a free tour at the Center for Kentucky History). An exhibit that tells the story of Kentucky's military engagements, both from historical and personal perspectives, is slated to become the permanent exhibit at the Military History Museum in the near future. Check with the Center for Kentucky History for updates.

Capital City Museum

Housed in the former Capital Hotel, which dates to the 1850s, the Capital City Museum (325 Ann St., 502/696-0607, www.frankfortparksandrec.com, 10 A.M.–4 P.M. Mon.–Sat., free) presents the story of Frankfort, from the founding of the town on the Kentucky River to its successful bid to become the state capital to its current state. Photos, artifacts, and life-size dioramas make the history accessible and interesting.

Liberty Hall Historic Site

Built at the end of the 18th century for U.S. Senator John Brown, Liberty Hall (202 Wilkinson St., 502/227-2560, www.libertyhall.org, tours at 10:30 A.M., noon, 1:30 P.M., 3 P.M. Tues.–Sat., spring–fall, $4 adults, $3 seniors, $1 youth 5–18) was one of the first brick buildings in Frankfort and remains an important landmark. The neighboring Orlando Brown House, though built in the Greek revival style, also belonged to Senator Brown, who had it built in 1835 so that each of his sons would inherit a house. Today hour-long tours take visitors through both properties, with guides helping to interpret history, architecture, and decor through the story of the Brown family. The tour doesn't include the grounds, but you should pad your schedule so that you have time to wander the lawn and gardens, which lead down to the Kentucky River.

Berry Mansion

Once owned by a wealthy family involved in the whiskey industry, the 22-room Berry Mansion (700 Louisville Rd., 502/564-3000, www.historicproperties.ky.gov, 8:30 A.M.–4 P.M. Mon.–Fri., free), built from stone quarried on the property, now houses government offices and hosts special events, including weddings. The first floor, however, is open to the public with a self-guided tour brochure pointing out highlights of the foyer, dining room, library, drawing room, music room, service wing, and grounds. Go ahead and gawk at the large pipe organ in the ornate music room; that room alone, which was added in 1912, cost nearly as much as the entire Governor's Mansion.

Frankfort Cemetery

Though governors, artists, military heroes, and the developer of Bibb lettuce all rest at Frankfort Cemetery (215 E. Main St., 502/227-2403, dawn–dusk), the burial ground's most famous residents are the Boones: Daniel and his wife Rebecca. Though both Boones died and were buried in Missouri, they were later brought back to Kentucky and interred in Frankfort in 1845. A tall rectangular monument, which stands on a bluff overlooking the Kentucky River and the capitol, marks their shared grave. Pick up a map and brochure at the information center or just follow the signs to Daniel Boone's grave.

BOURBON SIGHTS
☾ Buffalo Trace Distillery

Thanks to the fact that it was allowed to remain open during Prohibition as one of four distilleries authorized to produce "medicinal" liquor, Buffalo Trace Distillery (1001 Wilkinson Blvd., 502/696-5926, www.buffalotrace.com, tours on the hour 9 A.M.–3 P.M. Mon.–Fri., 10 A.M.–2 P.M. Sat., free) owns the title of the oldest continually operating distillery in America. A tour of Buffalo Trace starts with a short video that relays the history of the region and the distillery; continues with a peek at Warehouse D, where the 13 different bourbons made at the distillery are aged;

bourbon aging in a warehouse at Buffalo Trace Distillery

bald eagle at Salato Wildlife Education Center

segues into a visit to the line where premium bourbons are hand-bottled; and ends with a tasting, where you can choose two tastes from a selection that will include a couple of bourbons and may also include Rain, the vodka made on premises; White Dog Mash, the whiskey that the bourbon begins as; and other spirits made at the distillery.

In addition to the standard tour, Buffalo Trace also offers a Hard Hat Tour (Mon.– Sat. Sept.–June, by reservation), which shows the step-by-step process by which bourbon is made—from grain delivery through fermentation and distillation. Architecture and history aficionados will want to sign up for the Post Prohibition Tour (Mon.–Sat., by reservation) which focuses on the growth that took place at Buffalo Trace from 1930 to 1950 as Americans were once again allowed to legally consume alcohol.

Rebecca Ruth Candy Tours

Thanks to the creation of the now famous bourbon ball, Rebecca Ruth Candy (112 E. 2nd St., 502/223-7475, www.rebeccaruth.stores.yahoo.net, 10 A.M.–5:30 P.M. Mon.–Sat. Apr.–Nov., $2) products are enjoyed around the country and even internationally. The business didn't start out with such global aspirations, however. Instead it was founded by two substitute schoolteachers, Ruth Hanly and Rebecca Gooch, who decided they had more of a knack for making candy than for teaching. My sweet tooth agrees. Take a 20-minute tour of the small facility (which somehow manages to produce over three million pieces of candy each year) to learn about the history of the business and the women, see the century-old stove where candy is made, and hear the story of how an offhand comment led to the development of their signature candy. Samples are included on the tour.

OTHER SIGHTS
Salato Wildlife Education Center

Run by the Department of Fish and Wildlife, the Salato Wildlife Education Center

KENTUCKY'S DRY COUNTIES

As the number one producer of America's only native spirit, Kentucky appears on the surface to be a state that likes its liquor. Dive deeper, and you'll see that alcohol sales are a contentious issue in the Bluegrass State. After all, Carrie Nation, the radical hatchet-wielding leader of the temperance movement, was a Kentuckian.

Though most Americans consider it their right in post-Prohibition America to buy alcohol anywhere so long as they are of legal age, that's not the case in Kentucky. Only 32 of Kentucky's 120 counties are wet, meaning that alcoholic beverages can be sold by businesses for on-site or off-site consumption. A surprising 44 counties are completely dry, meaning alcohol sales are prohibited throughout the entire county. The remaining 44 counties are primarily dry, but may have a city that is completely wet (such as Bowling Green in Warren County), have cities that allow sales by the drink in certain restaurants, or have golf courses or wineries that are allowed to serve alcohol.

Dry areas can be found in every region in the state, though they are most concentrated in southern, eastern, and far western Kentucky, which are Bible Belt areas, and the ban on alcohol has everything to do with religious beliefs. In these areas, especially, you'll have to go a long way before you find alcohol, at least legal alcohol that is. Moonshine is alive and well in Kentucky, despite what officials may try to tell you. It should be noted that it is not illegal to possess alcohol for private consumption in dry counties; it is simply illegal to sell it. The majority of the wet counties are in the vicinity of Louisville, Lexington, Northern Kentucky, and Owensboro. Not only are these the state's most populated and urban areas, they also have strong Catholic communities. Interpret that how you will.

A map showing the distribution of wet and dry counties is available through the website of the Kentucky Department of Alcoholic Beverage Control (http://abc.ky.gov).

(1 Sportsman Ln., 502/564-7863, http://fw.ky.gov, 9 A.M.–5 P.M. Tues.–Fri., 10 A.M.–5 P.M. Sat., free) seeks to teach visitors about Kentucky ecosystems and the creation and protection of wildlife habitats. Start your visit in the exhibition hall, where you can check out live snakes, frogs, and fish, and dioramas of larger stuffed animals. Then hit the paved path for a circuit that will take you through a diversity of habitats and past large, natural enclosures housing eagles, black bears, elk, bison, bobcats, and deer. Those looking for a little more adventure will want to lace up their hiking books and explore the 0.5-mile red-blazed HabiTrek Trail, which connects with the 0.2-mile yellow-blazed Prairie Trail, or try out the three-mile white-blazed Pea Ridge Loop Trail. The complex also offers two fishing lakes and picnic areas, so pack your lunch and make it a day.

Kentucky State University

Created in 1886 to provide higher education to Kentucky's African Americans, Kentucky State University (400 E. Main St., 502/597-6000, www.kysu.edu) remains proud of its heritage while now serving a diverse student body. Visitors to the campus will want to stop in the Jackson Hall gallery and lobby, as well as the Visitor and Information Center in the Carroll Academic Services building to see rotating exhibitions culled from the collections of the Center of Excellence for the Study of Kentucky African Americans. A Kentucky Civil Rights Hall of Fame, which honors 52 inductees, can be viewed in the Carl Hill Student Center Ballroom. Campus maps are available at the Visitor and Information Center.

Kentucky Vietnam Veterans Memorial

The Kentucky Vietnam Veterans Memorial (300 Coffee Tree Rd., www.kyvietnammemorial.net) honors the 125,000 Kentuckians who served in the conflict, including the 1,103 who were killed. The design, by architect and veteran Helm Roberts, is unusual: the memorial is a very large sundial. The base, which is granite, is inscribed with the names of those who lost their lives and is patterned in such a way that on the anniversary of their death, the shadow of the sundial pointer falls on their name. Verses from Ecclesiastes are also inscribed in the base.

Frank Lloyd Wright's Ziegler House

Architecture fans will want to drive by the Ziegler House (509 Shelby St.), which was designed by architect Frank Lloyd Wright in his famous prairie house style. Though the clean-lined, white house is distinctive, it fits in seamlessly on the street, on which a number of impressive houses of varying styles are located. A historical marker indicates the house, which is private and may only be viewed from the street. The Ziegler House is the only Wright-designed house in Kentucky.

Switzer Covered Bridge

One of only a handful of remaining covered bridges in Kentucky, the Switzer Covered Bridge (KY 1262 & KY 1689), is a 120-foot-long Howe truss bridge built in 1855 to span the Elkhorn River. In 1954, the bridge was closed to traffic, a concrete structure taking its place. Restored multiple times since its construction, the bridge can now be crossed by foot, and though the external structure is in good condition, graffiti scars the interior.

ENTERTAINMENT AND EVENTS
Nightlife

Frankfort is not really known for its nightlife. Many government workers head back to their hometowns on weekends, while locals often opt to see what's going on in nearby Lexington. Stand-alone bars are few and far between, but many restaurants buzz in the evenings with locals seeking out a drink and entertainment. The bar at Serafini, for instance, is always crowded.

BARDSTOWN

© THERESA DOWELL BLACKINTON

Frank Lloyd Wright's Ziegler House

The hottest place in town for a drink is **Capital Cellars** (227 W. Broadway, 502/352-2600, 10 A.M.–9 P.M. Mon.–Thurs., 10 A.M.–10 P.M. Fri.–Sat.). It's where people come together, especially those interested in arts, culture, and meeting new friends. With an enormous selection of wines at reasonable prices ($4–6 per glass, a bottle can be enjoyed in-store for $2 over retail), as well as a short menu of sandwiches, salads, and snacks, such as cheese plates, olive trays, and smoked salmon, it's a great place to grab a light dinner, then hang out, as art exhibitions open, musicians start impromptu jam sessions, and people meet and mingle. For those not inclined toward wine, Capital Cellars also offers 35 Kentucky bourbons as well as a wide choice of other drinks.

Though the **Kentucky Coffeetree Café** (235 W. Broadway, 502/875-3009, www.kentuckycoffeetree.com, 7 A.M.–9 P.M. Mon.–Wed., 7 A.M.–11 P.M. Thurs.–Fri., 8 A.M.–11 P.M. Sat., 8 A.M.–7 P.M. Sun.) serves up coffees, smoothies, sandwiches, and pastries during the day, on weekend evenings it's the place to go for live music. The intimate setting makes it feel as if the musicians are playing just for you. Some performances are ticketed; others require a cover. Check the website for details.

For a more traditional bar experience, grab at table at **The Dragon Pub** (103 W. Main St., 502/875-9300, www.dragonpub.com, 11 A.M.–2 A.M. Mon.–Fri., 10 A.M.–1 A.M. Sat.), where Tuesday night is trivia night and Fridays feature live music. As the only Irish bar in town, The Dragon Pub celebrates St. Patrick's Day with gusto, though Halloween also gets its due. Expect a young professional crowd, ready to relax after work.

Performing Arts

Built in 1911 as a small vaudeville theater, the **Grand Theatre** (308 St. Clair St., 502/352-7469, www.grandtheatrefrankfort.org) was converted into a large movie theater in the 1940s before closing in 1966. Now, thanks to a group of activist citizens, the Grand is back as a community arts center. In addition to again showing films, the theater also hosts art exhibitions,

concerts, and other performances. Check the online schedule for upcoming events and ticket information.

Festivals and Events

If it's 7 P.M. on a Friday in the summer, head to the lawn of the Old State Capitol for the **Family Summer Concert Series** (www.downtownfrankfort.com). Bring a blanket, bring a friend, bring a picnic; entertainment is provided.

On the first weekend of June, Frankfort shows off its goods at the **Capitol Expo Festival** (www.capitalexpofestival.com). The three-day event includes a cornhole tournament, Frankfort Idol, a fireworks show over the Kentucky River, an arts and crafts show, and lots of live music.

SHOPPING
Bookstores

Bookstore lovers will delight in **Poor Richard's Books** (233 W. Broadway, 502/223-8018, www.poorrichards.booksense.com, 9:30 A.M.–6 P.M. Mon.–Fri., 9:30 A.M.–5 P.M. Sat., 12:30–5 P.M. Sun.), where the front shelves are dedicated to Kentucky authors while the rest of the store contains popular offerings in every genre. It's nearly impossible to leave without a new read in hand.

Kentucky Products

From horse brooches to carved wooden benches, **Completely Kentucky** (237 W. Broadway, 502/223-5240, www.completelykentucky.com, 9:30 A.M.–6 P.M. Mon.–Fri., 9:30 A.M.–5 P.M. Sat., 12:30–5 P.M. Sun.) covers the entire spread of Kentucky-made arts, crafts, and souvenirs. Items range from the decorative (glass pieces and prints) to the useful (ceramic dishes) to the mouthwatering (gift baskets of Kentucky food) to the absurd (junkyard animals). There's something for everyone.

For other unique, local products be sure to check out the gift shops at the Center for Kentucky History and Buffalo Trace Distillery.

SPORTS AND RECREATION
Parks
Stop at **River View Park** (Wilkinson Blvd., across from Capital Plaza) for a walk along a one-mile path that runs parallel to the Kentucky River. Sixteen sites of historical interest are marked along the trail. The park also offers a fishing pier, boat dock, and picnic area, and hosts the farmers market May–October.

Juniper Hill Park (800 Louisville Rd., 502/696-0607, www.frankfortparksandrec. com, 7 A.M.–11 P.M. Apr.–Oct., 7 A.M.–dark Nov.–Mar.) offers some of the best recreational facilities in the city with an Olympic-size pool, sand volleyball courts, tennis courts, and 18-hole golf course. You'll also find extensive picnic facilities and a playground at Juniper Hill.

Pull over at the **scenic overlook** on U.S. 60 as you head out of downtown Frankfort and go toward Louisville for an excellent view of the capitol, which sits directly in front of and below the overlook.

Hiking
Start your visit to **Cove Spring Park** (100 Cove Spring Rd., 502/696-0607, www.frankfortparksandrec.com, 8 A.M.–11 P.M. Apr.–Oct., 8 A.M.–dark Nov.–Mar.) with a stop at the waterfall located right next to the parking lot, then create a hiking route from the park's four trails and multiple connectors. No matter what path you choose to use to explore the park's 100 acres, you'll pass through riverine forest that is home to deer, wild turkeys, great blue herons, and other wildlife.

From Fort Hill, Frankfort militia protected the city from an attempted Confederate invasion in 1864. Today, **Leslie Morris Park** (400 Clifton Ave., 502/696-0607, www.frankfortparksandrec.com, dawn–dusk daily) preserves the remains of the forts built on this hill and allows visitors to experience them on a series of trails that loop through acres of forest, where deer and other wildlife are known to live. A brochure available from a box in the parking lot outlines a 0.6-mile route that takes you past many of the sites and provides a wonderful panorama of the entirety of Frankfort. Those looking for a good workout can actually ascend the hill from the city via the Old Military Road Walking Trail, which begins behind the Capital Plaza tower.

Biking
Capital City Cycles (475 Versailles Rd., 502/352-2480, www.capitalcitycyclesweb. com, 10 A.M.–6 P.M. Mon.–Sat., noon–5 P.M. Sun.) is Frankfort's go-to place for all biking needs. The shop services and sells bikes and also rents road, mountain, and hybrid bikes by the day and week. Staff members are avid cyclists and can answer any question you have about where to bike in Frankfort. Check their website or visit the store for maps of popular road and off-road routes that range in length and difficulty. If you like to ride with others or want to learn the route from experienced cyclists, be at the store at 6 P.M. on Thursday for a group ride.

In addition to soccer and softball fields, **Capitol View Park** (Glenns Creek Rd., 502/696-0607, www.frankfortparksandrec.com,

waterfall at Cove Spring Park

© THERESA DOWELL BLACKINTON

BARDSTOWN

8 A.M.–11 P.M. Apr.–Oct., 8 A.M.–dark Nov.–Mar.) features 10 miles of mountain bike trails. The trails run along the river and through the woods and connect to make one large loop. A map of the trails can be found on the park website or picked up at Capital City Cycles.

Water Sports

The Kentucky River and Elkhorn Creek offer excellent canoeing and kayaking waters, and there's no outfitter better suited to help get you out on those waters than **Canoe Kentucky** (7323 Peaks Mill Rd., 888/226-6359, www.canoeky.com). They offer instruction for those new to the activity, sales for those who can't get enough, and both guided and self-guided boat trips for paddlers of all levels. Kentucky River trips include a by-the-hour paddling tour of the downtown area (Sat.–Sun. May–Nov.) as well as a two-hour sunset tour. Outings on the Elkhorn include 6- and 12-mile fun floats through Class I waters, a 7-mile run through Class II–III rapids, a 13-mile combo trip, and a selection of fishing trips. Children are welcome as long as they weigh over 35 pounds. All activities should be booked in advance.

Horseback Riding

A Little Bit of Heaven Riding Stables (3226 Sullivan Ln., 502/223-8925, www.kystable.com) offers horseback riding lessons on their Appaloosa horses. No experience is necessary, but you do need to call ahead to arrange a lesson. Because of the size of the horses, a weight limit of 185 pounds is strictly enforced. Those too timid to climb onboard are welcome to take a tour of the paddock and meet the nearly 50 horses boarded there.

ACCOMMODATIONS
$50-100

The **Capital Plaza Hotel** (405 Wilkinson Blvd., 502/227-5100, www.capitalplazaky.com, $85–95) offers 189 guest rooms outfitted with standard hotel amenities, including cable television and wireless Internet, and decorated in standard hotel style. Located next to the convention center, the hotel is popular with business travelers, but it is also within walking distance of Frankfort's main sights. For those who like to know what they're going to get in a hotel, the Capital Plaza delivers a clean, comfortable room in a good location at a fair price.

A number of chain hotels are located in Frankfort, including a **Hampton Inn** (1310 U.S. 127 S, 502/223-7600, www.hamptoninn.com, $99) and a **Best Western** (80 Chenault Dr., 502/695-6111, www.bestwesternkentucky.com, $79–89), both of which offer nice rooms with all the amenities one would expect. While each is convenient to I-64, neither is located in the heart of the city.

$100-150

Built prior to the Civil War, **[The Meeting House Bed and Breakfast** (519 Ann St., 502/226-3226, www.themeetinghousebandb.com, $115–125) retains many of the features of the original building, including the poplar floors, the walnut banister on the three-floor staircase, the high ceilings, and the many fireplaces. Period pieces throughout the house, which is located within easy walking distance of most attractions, add to the historic feel. The house has been updated, however, so that each of the four guest rooms has its own private bath with walk-in shower. Rooms are large with desks and comfortable chairs and feature cable TV and wireless Internet. Three rooms have full beds and one has a queen. Homemade cookies are served each afternoon, and breakfast is served in courses. Scottish eggs are the house specialty. Don't let the Boston accent of hosts Gary and Rose throw you; they know more about Frankfort than many of its life-long residents.

The bathroom attached to the Red Room at **Meek House Bed and Breakfast** (119 E. 3rd St., 502/227-2566, www.bbonline.com, $110) was, in its last incarnation, most likely a bedroom. It's that big. It features a claw foot tub and walk-in shower and even has its own door to the patio overlooking the tranquil garden. The bedroom is itself quite large, with plenty of open space left despite the room having a king-size bed and loveseat. The B&B's other room, the Green Room, is perfect for traveling partners who prefer separate beds as it contains two twins as well as a pull-out couch. Both rooms have stocked refrigerators and TVs. At the multi-course breakfast, you might be treated to a Mexican quiche, herbed eggs with cheese on an English muffin, or cinnamon chip French toast, as well as a starter course of yogurt and homemade granola.

Campgrounds

RVers will be happy with the services at **Elkhorn Campground** (165 N. Scruggs Ln., 502/695-9154, www.elkhorncampground. com), which offers 125 sites, 61 of which have full hook-ups. For entertainment choose between the campground's pool, mini-golf facility, horseshoe pit, basketball and volleyball courts, and playground. Located on the banks of the Elkhorn, the location is peaceful as well as convenient to Frankfort sites.

Those more interested in outdoor offerings than historic sites will want to check out **Still Waters Campground** (249 Strohmeier Rd., 502/223-8896, www.stillwaterscampground. com), which is located on the Kentucky River and features boat ramps and offers canoe and kayak rentals. In addition to full service sites, the campground also has two primitive camping areas.

FOOD
Farmers Market

Fresh fruits, vegetables, and assorted other agricultural products are available for purchase at the Frankfort Farmers Market four times each week (River View Park, 7 A.M. to sellout Tues., Thurs., Sat., and 3:30–7:30 P.M. Wed.).

Bakeries and Cafés

Candleberry's Tea Room & Café (1502 Louisville Rd., 502/875-0485, www.candleberrytearoom.com, 11 A.M.–2 P.M. Mon–Fri., noon–3 P.M. Sat., $5.95–7.95) offers light lunches served in a cozy atmosphere. Take your pick from a list of sandwiches or daily quiche and soup specials. If you can't decide, they'll

let you mix and match. Finish your meal with a perfectly sweet piece of chess pie, said to be made from a vintage recipe. Of course, you'll want to have tea with your meal—only trouble is you have to pick from a long, tempting list. For the true tea connoisseur, book a reservation for afternoon tea on Saturday, where you'll be treated to scones, soup, and a selection of sweet and savory goodies to go along with your tea. It's perfect for an outing with the girls or a mother-daughter date, though men are plenty welcome.

Gourmet sandwiches make up the menu at **Clare Ann's** (241 W. Main St., 502/352-2725, www.clareanns.com, 8:30 A.M.–3 P.M. Mon.–Fri., $6–8), a chic spot with high ceilings and tall tables. Turkey, roast beef, country ham, pimento cheese, and other lunch favorites are sandwiched between slices of homemade sourdough, oatmeal walnut, and other delicious breads. Add a side of pasta salad or Caribbean couscous salad or do a half-and-half with potato leek soup or a baby blue salad. If it's looking like a good day for a picnic, Clare Ann's offers box lunches to go.

For a breakfast treat or an afternoon sweet, visit **Magee's Bakery** (225 W. Main, 502/223-7621, 7:30 A.M.–5 P.M. Tues.–Fri., 8 A.M.–1 P.M. Sat., $1–4) and choose from a tasty selection of fresh baked goodies.

American

Though a few pasta and meat entrées dot the menu at lunch with a couple more added at dinner, **Gibby's** (204 W. Broadway, 502/223-4429, www.eatatgibbys.com, 10:30 A.M.–9 P.M. Mon.–Fri., 10:30 A.M.–8 P.M. Sat., $4.99–12.99) primarily sticks to what it's known for: filling sandwiches and stuffed spuds. Located in the revitalized downtown, Gibby's does a bustling lunch business, popular with locals looking for a quick, tasty lunch before heading back to work.

Italian

Buddy's Pizza (212 W. Broadway, 502/352-2920, 11 A.M.–9 P.M. Mon.–Thurs., 11 A.M.–10 P.M. Fri., noon–9 P.M. Sat., $8–17.50) offers the best pies in town. Choose from a specialty pizza or create your own combo to be baked to perfection in Buddy's brick oven. Salads and Italian sandwiches ($4–7) round out the menu. At lunch on weekdays, pizza is available by the slice ($2.50).

Serafini (243 W. Broadway, 502/875-5599, 11 A.M.–3 P.M. and 4:30–10 P.M. Mon.–Sat., $21–39) is Frankfort's nicest restaurant, serving up an excellent selection of pastas and meat dishes. Choose from steaks, pork tenderloin, veal meatballs with tagliatelle, or the risotto of the day. Add a side salad at your own risk; eat it with the complimentary bread with oil and vinegar and you might be full before your entrée arrives. You'll want to try to save room for dessert, though you'll probably want to split one of the rich creations. Complement any meal with a drink made to order by Seneca at the bar; just tell him what you're having and he'll create the perfect match (perhaps built around one of their nearly 90 bourbons). Tall booths provide privacy, though you can also opt for an open table or even open air seating when the weather is nice.

INFORMATION AND SERVICES

Located in a beautiful Queen Anne style house, the **Visitors Center** (100 Capital Ave., 502/875-8687, www.visitfrankfort.com, 8 A.M.–5 P.M. Mon.–Fri., 9:30 A.M.–2:30 P.M. Sat. May–Sept.) stocks brochures and maps, and the friendly staff can provide you with information on dining and hotel options in Frankfort and Franklin County. The center also offers free wireless Internet.

A **post office** is located at 1210 Wilkinson Boulevard, near Buffalo Trace Distillery.

GETTING THERE

Frankfort is located just north of I-64. From Louisville, take eastbound I-64 for nearly 50 miles to northbound U.S. 127 (Exit 53B), which will lead into downtown Frankfort after about five miles. From Lexington, you can take westbound I-64 for 21 miles to westbound U.S. 60 (Exit 58). After 2.5 miles

U.S. 60 will hit Main Street. If you prefer to avoid the interstate or are on the western side of Lexington, drive 20 miles on northbound U.S. 421, at which point you'll hit Main Street. From Bardstown, travel on eastbound Martha Layne Collins Blue Grass Parkway for 34 miles to northbound U.S. 127 (Exit 59B). Then drive an additional 16 miles, passing through Lawrenceburg, to reach Frankfort.

Frankfort's Capital City Airport is not served by commercial airlines. The nearest airports are Blue Grass Airport in Lexington and Louisville International Airport.

GETTING AROUND
Public Transportation

Listen for the friendly ring of Frankfort's free **downtown trolley** (www.frankforttransit.com, 10 A.M.–3 P.M. Tues.–Fri.); then hop onboard to enjoy old-fashioned transport between the city's most popular sites. Among the many stops are the Capitol, Rebecca Ruth Candy, Frankfort Cemetery, The Center for Kentucky History, Liberty Hall, River View Park, and Buffalo Trace Distillery. Departures are scheduled at 40-minute intervals, making the trolley a fun and convenient way to see Frankfort.

Tours

Bluegrass Wine and Spirits (859/873-5122, www.bluegrasswineandspirits.com) leads three-day tours through Frankfort, Lawrenceburg, and Midway. The tours are centered around Kentucky's wine and bourbon industries, and include visits to distilleries and wineries along with stops at nearby historic sites.

Multiple walking tours of Frankfort are offered throughout the year. During the summer months of June through September, **Russ Hatter's Downtown Tour** departs the Capital City Museum at 10:30 A.M. on Tuesdays and Thursdays. The walking tour, which costs $5 for adults and is free for those under 12, provides an in-depth look at Frankfort history. Those who delight in the fact that trains still run right through Frankfort will be interested in **Chuck Bogart's Railroad Walking Tour,** an hour-long trip through railroad history. The tour, held on Tuesdays in September, are free and depart from the L&N depot across from the Capital City Museum at 6:30 P.M. Reservations can be made by calling 502/227-2436. Naturalists will want to sign up for **Russ Kennedy's Kentucky River Walk,** which departs from River View Park on the last Thursday of the month June–September at 10:30 A.M. Sign up for the walking tour, which costs $5 for adults and is free for youth under 12, by calling 502/803-0242. If you're visiting Frankfort during the witching month, get in the mood for Halloween with a **Murder and Mayhem Tour,** held every Thursday night in October at 7:30 P.M. Guides, costumed like early 20th-century policemen, tell tales of 30 grisly Frankfort murders while leading a tour through the nighttime streets of Frankfort. The tour, which costs $10 and departs from the Capital City Museum, is restricted to those 18 and older. Reserve a spot on the tour by calling 502/696-0607.

For those who prefer to tour at their own pace, walking and driving tour brochures are available at the visitors center. To uncover the stories behind the many historic buildings that form the heart of downtown Frankfort, request a copy of the **walking tour brochure.** Brief histories of 40 different sites, all within a 10-block radius, are provided in the brochure. Civil War buffs will want to pick up a copy of the **Civil War Driving Tour** brochure and follow the route to 15 sites with connections to the war. All sites are within the city, so driving distances are short but the tour is long on interesting facts.

BARDSTOWN

Versailles and Midway

Woodford County, home to the towns of Versailles and Midway, produces some of the finest products to come out of Kentucky—Woodford Reserve bourbon and thoroughbred racehorses. Both the towns are small but wealthy and offer food and accommodation of a quality that far exceeds their size. Versailles, which is pronounced Vur-sales since this is Kentucky and not France, is the bigger of the two cities, named in honor of General Lafayette, a friend of the city's founder. Midway, which isn't much more than a main street and a whole lot of surrounding farmland, was Kentucky's first railroad town. It is strategically situated midway (hence its name) between Frankfort and Lexington. Both towns are exceedingly charming, and the drive between the two is on a scenic byway lined with gorgeous horse farms. Very close to Lexington, either city makes a good base for exploring the entire region.

HORSE FARMS

Woodford County is home to over 100 horse farms. At times, while driving around the area, it can seem as if there is nothing else. Everywhere your gaze falls, you'll find stone and wood fences enclosing rolling bluegrass hills dotted with horses. The majority of the farms are closed to the public, though those listed here welcome visitors with advance reservations.

Ashford Stud

Derby winners Fusaichi Pegasus and Thunder Gulch are two of the stallions that stand in the distinctive blue-trimmed barns at Ashford Stud (5095 Frankfort Rd., Versailles, 859/873-7088, www.coolmore.com). Free tours of the breeding complex at this beautiful facility are offered by reservation. The horses may travel south during the latter half of the year, so aim to visit Ashford Stud between February and June if possible.

Lane's End

Outside of the breeding season, Lane's End (1500 Midway Rd., Versailles, 859/873-7300, www.lanesend.com, 10 A.M. Thurs. July–Jan.) offers free tours of their stallion complex. Meet the horses, learn about the industry, and admire Lane's End's park-like setting. Among the more well-known horses on-site is Curlin, a two-time Horse of the Year. The facility hosts a couple of open houses each year, which are open to both breeders and the public. Check the website to find out if an open house is on the schedule.

Three Chimneys Farm

Three Chimneys Farm (1981 Old Frankfort Pike, Versailles, 859/873-7053, www.threechimneys.com, 1 P.M. Tues.–Sat., $10) has been home to a long list of thoroughbreds that any horse racing fan will know, including Seattle Slew, Silver Charm, Genuine Risk, Big Brown, and Smarty Jones. The last two are currently standing stud at Three Chimneys Farm and are often brought out and walked for visitors. If a breeding session is scheduled during your visit, you may be allowed to watch. With notable stone architecture and lush green fields, Three Chimneys Farm is not just a premier stud farm but also a pretty place to tour.

WinStar Farm

For an insider's look at how champion thoroughbred horses are bred, visit WinStar Farm (3301 Pisgah Pike, Versailles, 859/873-1717, www.winstarfarm.com, 1 P.M. Mon., Wed., and Fri.), owner of 2010 Kentucky Derby winner Super Saver. Tours begin with a video that features 2000 Horse of the Year Tiznow. Visitors then move into the stallion complex, where they are introduced to the farm's stallions, including attention-loving Tiznow, and are informed about the process of breeding. Guides can answer any and all questions you might have about thoroughbreds, racing, breeding, sales, and training, so don't be shy. Free tours

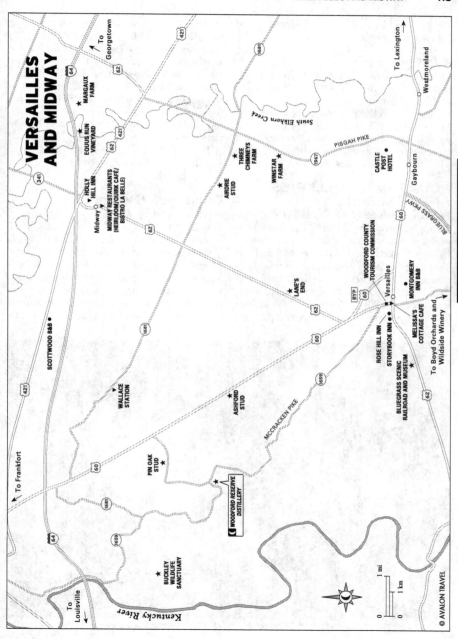

VERSAILLES AND MIDWAY

BARDSTOWN

To Georgetown

To Lexington

Westmoreland

South Elkhorn Creek

PISGAH PIKE

MARGAUX FARM

EQUUS RUN VINEYARD

HOLLY HILL INN

Midway

MIDWAY RESTAURANTS (HEIRLOOM/QUIRK CAFÉ/ BISTRO LA BELLE)

THREE CHIMNEYS FARM

AIRDRIE STUD

WINSTAR FARM

CASTLE POST HOTEL

Gaybourn

BLUEGRASS PKWY

WOODFORD COUNTY TOURISM COMMISSION

Versailles

BYP

LANE'S END

MONTGOMERY INN B&B

ROSE HILL INN

STORYBOOK INN

MELISSA'S COTTAGE CAFÉ

BLUEGRASS SCENIC RAILROAD AND MUSEUM

To Boyd Orchards and Wildside Winery

SCOTTWOOD B&B

WALLACE STATION

ASHFORD STUD

McCRACKEN PIKE

PIN OAK STUD

WOODFORD RESERVE DISTILLERY

To Frankfort

BUCKLEY WILDLIFE SANCTUARY

To Louisville

Kentucky River

1 mi

1 km

© AVALON TRAVEL

are offered at 1 P.M. Monday, Wednesday, and Friday by reservation.

Additional Farms

Other horse farms that provide free tours of their facilities include **Airdrie Stud** (2641 Old Frankfort Pike, Midway, 859/873-7270, www.airdriestud.com), **Margaux Farm** (596 Moore's Mill Rd., Versailles, 859/846-4433, www.margauxfarm.com), and **Pin Oak Stud** (830 Grassy Springs Rd., Versailles, 859/873-1420, www.pinoakstud.com).

BOURBON DISTILLERIES AND WINERIES
Woodford Reserve Distillery

Though Woodford Reserve has been produced only since 1996, the National Historic Landmark distillery (7855 McCracken Pike, Versailles, 859/879-1812, www.woodfordreserve.com, 9 A.M.–5 P.M. Tues.–Sat., year-round, 12:30–4:30 P.M. Sun. Apr.–Oct.) where it is made is one of the oldest distilleries in the state. Join a one-hour tour for an in-depth look at the process by which this premium bourbon, the official bourbon of the Kentucky Derby, is made. You'll see the only stone aging warehouses in America, learn that Woodford Reserve is the only bourbon to be distilled three times before being barreled, and visit the only bourbon fermenting facility to use wood tanks exclusively. Tours end with a tasting, and visitors are allowed to take their shot glass home with them. Tours ($5) are offered at 10 A.M., 11 A.M., 1 P.M., 2 P.M., and 3 P.M. Tuesday–Saturday, and at 1 P.M., 2 P.M., and 3 P.M. Sunday.

Equus Run Vineyards

Nestled between horse farms and South Elkhorn Creek, Equus Run Vineyards (1280 Moores Mill Rd., Midway, 859/846-9463, www.equusrunvineyards.com, 11 A.M.–7 P.M. Mon.–Sat. Apr.–Oct., 11 A.M.–5 P.M. Mon.–Sat. Nov.–Mar.) has been producing award-winning wines since 1998. Vineyard guests are welcome to take a self-guided tour of the grounds followed by a tasting ($2). The

grains used in the production of bourbon at Woodford Reserve Distillery

© THERESA DOWELL BLACKINTON

vineyard produces 10 red, white, and rosé wines, and as the official wine of the Derby, also creates special edition wines each year. A number of events are held at the vineyard, including a very popular summer concert series. Check the website for a schedule of upcoming events.

Wildside Winery

Wildside Winery (5500 Troy Pike, Versailles, 859/321-5046, www.wildsidevines.com, 1–7 P.M. Tues.–Sat., 1–5 P.M. Sun.) makes a long list of wines, focusing especially on dry red wines and sweet fruit wines. In addition to the usual strawberry and blackberry wine, Wildside also does peach mead and cranberry and cherry wine plus a few other less common selections. Among the reds, you'll find a syrah, a cabernet sauvignon, and a Cynthiana, along with a bourbon barrel red, which is a cabernet that is aged in a bourbon barrel. A couple of whites are also available, including a sparkling pear-apple wine. Tastings are free, and the winery occasionally hosts outdoor concerts.

OTHER SIGHTS
Bluegrass Scenic Railroad and Museum

Get a taste of rail travel on a one-hour train ride with Bluegrass Scenic Railroad and Museum (175 Beasley Rd., Versailles, 859/873-2476, www.bluegrassrailroad.com, 1–4 P.M. weekends). The rides, which are offered at 2 P.M. on weekends mid-May–October, take passengers through the bluegrass countryside. You'll pass through Trackside Farm, where thoroughbreds are raised, and see cattle, tobacco fields, and other rural Kentucky sites. Special train rides are held throughout the year and include Civil War train robbery rides, mystery theater rides, haunted Halloween rides, and a Christmas ride with Santa. Come early or hang around after the ride to explore the one-room museum, which has exhibits on the jobs the railroad did for the United States, the jobs of those who worked for the railroad, and the trains that used to pass through the area. Tickets ($10 adults, $9 seniors, $8 youth 2–12)

can be purchased online or in person. Plan to arrive 30 minutes before departure, because trains here run on a Swiss timetable, departing right on schedule.

Boyd Orchards

As fifth-generation fruit growers, the Boyd family knows a little something about fruit, and a visit to Boyd Orchards (1386 Pinckard Pike, Versailles, 859/873-3097, www.boydorchards.com, 9 A.M.–6 P.M. Tues.–Thurs., 9 A.M.–9 P.M. Fri.–Sat., noon–6 P.M. Sun.) is a treat for your taste buds. The only problem is that after tasting their strawberries, peaches, apples, blackberries, raspberries, grapes, and pears, you might be too spoiled to ever again settle for grocery store produce. Beyond producing mouthwatering fruit that you can purchase already picked or head to the fields to pick yourself, Boyd Orchards also has an enormous playground that kids love and a great gift shop full of unique products. During the seven weeks leading up to Halloween, Boyd Orchards hosts an extremely popular fall festival with a petting zoo, live music, corn maze, face painting, pony rides, mini train rides, hayrides, and of course, plenty of pumpkins, mums, and gourds. Their **Apple Blossom Café** has a full kitchen that turns out tasty lunches that often feature fruit fresh from the farm. Try the fruit slushes and the sandwiches and salads built around the produce of the moment (maybe a strawberry goat cheese salad or a Cuban sandwich with asparagus). For dessert, good luck choosing between apple cider doughnuts and fried apple or peach pies. In addition to lunch, the café also does a Friday night fish fry and a Saturday night barbecue.

SPORTS AND RECREATION
Hiking

The **Buckley Wildlife Sanctuary** (1305 Germany Rd., Versailles, 859/873-5711, www.audubon.org, 9 A.M.–5 P.M. Wed.–Fri., 9 A.M.–6 P.M. Sat.–Sun., $4 adults, $3 youth) has four trails, ranging in length from 0.3 mile to 1.5 miles and easily connectable, which lead into field, pond, and forest habitats. A bulletin board in the parking lot has a box filled with binders that provide information on the trails and point out sights you'll encounter along the way. Bird lovers will enjoy the bird blind, which is perched on the edge of a pond that many avian species like to visit. Field guides are provided for identification of species, but bring your own binoculars. From April through December, the Nature Center is open 1–6 P.M. weekends.

ACCOMMODATIONS

Versailles and Midway offer a surprising number of accommodation options, none of which are chains. With their close proximity to Lexington and especially Keeneland, the B&Bs in Versailles and Midway are a good option for those looking to spend time all around the region.

$150-200

Dating back to 1795, the house that is now ◖ **Scottwood Bed and Breakfast** (2004 Leestown Pike, Midway, 859/846-5037, www.scottwoodbb.com, $175–195) journeyed from its original location in Scott County to its present location in 1971. An addition was added at that point, but the house maintains the beautiful period woodwork and floors. Two guest rooms are located in the house, one on the main floor, the other occupying the entirety of the second floor. The upstairs suite, which can accommodate a family or group thanks to the twin beds in the room that adjoins the main bedroom, is decorated in Shaker style, while the down bedroom is done in the style of Williamsburg. Both rooms have private baths. A carriage house is located behind the main house and offers a private retreat with working fireplace and a lovely deck overlooking South Elkhorn Creek. Breakfast is provided each morning, and the rooms are equipped with satellite television and wireless Internet.

No one stays at ◖ **Rose Hill Inn** (233 Rose Hill Ave., Versailles, 859/873-5957, www.rosehillinn.com, $139–184) and doesn't love it. The seven tastefully decorated rooms in this historic 1823 home have private baths, comfy

beds, and TVs, and come with special touches like robes, homemade cookies, and candles. All rooms are spacious, and the various configurations—kings, queens, twins—can accommodate couples, families, or groups of friends. Some rooms feature whirlpool tubs and kitchen areas, and three of the rooms are even able to accommodate pets. The owners are excellent hosts who serve up a delicious breakfast daily and will do everything in their power to make sure you have a wonderful stay.

The **Montgomery Inn Bed and Breakfast** (270 Montgomery Ave., Versailles, 859/251-4103, www.montgomeryinnbnb.com, $139–179) has 10 guest suites, each with a private bathroom with whirlpool tub, queen or king bed, TV with DVD player, and Internet access. Some have private entryways, and all have access to complimentary snacks and drinks. Rates include a full breakfast. The decor can be a little bit busy, with patterned wallpapers, bed covers, and upholstery overwhelming those with simpler tastes. Those with allergies should be aware that multiple cats call the inn home.

Over $200

◖ **Storybook Inn** (277 Rose Hill Ave., Versailles, 859/879-9993, www.storybook-inn.com, $199–269) is an upscale bed-and-breakfast where not a single detail is overlooked. An antebellum style mansion dating to 1843, Storybook Inn was closed in 2009–2010 for updates and additions, though returning guests will find that it hasn't lost a bit of its charm. In the inn's three suites, you'll find such niceties as rain showerheads, soaking tubs, towel warmers, and fireplaces, not to mention luxurious linens, mattresses, and furniture. A cottage with two bedrooms, a kitchen, and a private deck is perfect for those seeking privacy or traveling in a group. Common areas include a beautiful garden and a library stocked with books and movies. Homemade treats and refreshments are available all day, and the delicious breakfasts can be tailored to accommodate any restrictions. Innkeeper Elise is a delight and will dedicate her full attention to helping you plan your visit.

It's impossible to drive down Pisgah Pike and not see the **Castle Post Hotel** (230 Pisgah Pike, Versailles, 859/879-1000, www.thecastle-post.com, $375–1,250). It is, after all, a castle with turrets, 12-foot wooden doors, and stone walls, smack in the middle of horse country. Though there are a lot of people who want to tour it, the only way you can gain admission to the castle is by booking an overnight room. It's not cheap—oh no, it's not—but hey, how many people can say they've slept in a castle in Kentucky? Rooms are luxuriously decorated (for better or worse, they don't feel at all medieval) and come with all the amenities. Shared facilities include a pool, tennis court, basketball court, but the grounds aren't as well manicured as you'd expect.

FOOD

You will not go hungry while visiting Versailles and Midway. Locally owned restaurants rule, and they're doing exciting things with food here.

Contemporary American

Details matter at **Heirloom** (125 E. Main St., Midway, 859/846-5565, www.heirloommidway.com, 11:30 A.M.–2 P.M. and 5:30 P.M.–close Tues.–Sat., $19–31). The dining room is elegant but comfortable, decorated in shades of brown, tan, and white and furnished with extra-tall booths and granite tables. Presentation is an art, with each dish expertly plated on unique dishes, and the tastes are spectacular. The menu is short, featuring about seven entrées, but each is carefully thought out and executed. The menu changes regularly, but the chile-roasted tiger prawns and the cucumber soup are both delicious. For a nice dinner out, you can't go wrong with Heirloom.

Holly Hill Inn (426 N. Winter St., Midway, 859/846-4732, www.hollyhill-inn.com, 11 A.M.–2 P.M. and 5:30–10 P.M. Wed.–Sun., $18–30) serves elevated Southern cuisine in an 1845 country inn. James Beard–nominated chef Ouita Michel prepares such excellent dishes as veal sweetbreads, squab with foie gras, and hazelnut-crusted flounder, using local products whenever possible. A three-course meal, in which you choose from a list of offerings, is served for lunch and Sunday brunch. Reservations are highly recommended at this deservedly popular restaurant.

Another notable fine dining option is **Bistro La Belle** (121 Main St., Midway, 859/846-4233, $17–30), which is open only Wednesday–Saturday for dinner. When the chef's in the kitchen, you'd do well to grab a table and see what's on the menu. The shrimp and grits are done in proper Low Country style, and the Hot Brown is a favorite. The bar does excellent cocktails, and desserts change daily.

Casual American

The Big Brown burger at **Wallace Station** (3854 Old Frankfort Pike, Versailles, 859/846-5161, www.wallacestation.com, 8 A.M.–8 P.M. Mon. and Fri., 8 A.M.–5 P.M. Tues.–Thurs. and Sat., 10 A.M.–4 P.M. Sun., $5.95–8.95) was named a top five burger by Guy Fieri of Food Network's *Diners, Drive-Ins, and Dives,* who visited this deli and bakery in 2010. If you're not into burgers, you can choose from a very long list of sandwiches, all of which are very good. Wallace Station is completely low-key with a few mismatched tables and chairs inside and a number of picnic tables on a deck. There's usually live music on Friday, and they're always busy at peak meal times.

Exclusively serving lunch, **Quirk Café** (131 E. Main St., Midway, 859/846-4688, www.quirkcafemidway.com, 11 A.M.–3 P.M. Tues.–Sun., $5.95–9.95) specializes in salads and sandwiches. It's a comfy place with local art on the walls and a lovely old tin ceiling. Live music complements meals, and if you're not in the market for a meal, you can just have dessert. Kentucky Silk Pie, a type of chocolate pie made in Midway and distributed throughout the state, is a good choice, but so is the jam cake or the bourbon and cream bread pudding.

Fans of comfort food will find refuge at **Melissa's Cottage Café** (167 S. Main St., Versailles, 859/879-6204, 11 A.M.–9 P.M. Mon.–Fri., 5–9 P.M. Sat., $6.95–11.95), where meatloaf, chicken pot pie, and hamburger steak

BARDSTOWN

© THERESA DOWELL BLACKINTON

Train tracks pass the restaurants of downtown Midway.

are some of the most popular entrées. Portions are generous and come with good Southern-style sides. The menu does change often and is presented to you on a chalkboard. Unlike many comfort food spots, Melissa's is a charming (albeit tiny) place with tasteful decor.

For a rather unusual dining experience, head out of town to a tiny place called Nonesuch, Kentucky, where you'll find an enormous antique gallery called Irish Acres. Proceed to the lower level to a restaurant named **The Glitz** (4205 Fords Mill Rd., Nonesuch, 859/873-7235, www.irishacresgallery.com, 11:30 A.M.–2:30 P.M. Tues.–Sat.), which makes complete sense when you see the place. The Glitz serves a three-course luncheon menu, with multiple selections for each of the courses. For dessert, you'll want to try the signature dish, the Nonesuch Pie, which involves a meringue shell, ice cream, chocolate sauce, whipped cream, almonds, and a cherry. The food is carefully prepared, and the atmosphere incomparable. Beverages are included with the meal, which costs $19.95. Reservations are required.

INFORMATION AND SERVICES

The **Woodford County Tourism Commission** (141 N. Main St., Versailles, 859/873-5122, www.woodfordcountyinfo.com) is run through the Chamber of Commerce. An information center is located in the front of the office.

GETTING THERE AND AROUND

Versailles is located directly west of Lexington on U.S. 60, which connects the two cities. From the center of Lexington, Versailles is about 13 miles away, though Versailles is only about six miles from Keeneland, making it equally as convenient if you're in the area for horse racing. Midway is north of Versailles, located just south of I-64. To travel between Versailles and Midway, drive 6.5 miles on westbound U.S. 62. From Lexington the most direct route to Midway is via northbound U.S. 421. Lexington and Midway are separated by 15 miles. From Louisville and points westward, take I-64 to Exit 58 to reach Versailles and Exit 65 to reach Midway.

www.moon.com

DESTINATIONS | ACTIVITIES | BLOGS | MAPS | BOOKS

MOON.COM is ready to help plan your next trip! Filled with fresh trip ideas and strategies, author interviews, informative travel blogs, a detailed map library, and descriptions of all the Moon guidebooks, Moon.com is all you need to get out and explore the world—or even places in your own backyard. While at Moon.com, sign up for our monthly e-newsletter for updates on new releases, travel tips, and expert advice from our on-the-go Moon authors. As always, when you travel with Moon, expect an experience that is uncommon and truly unique.

KEEP UP WITH MOON ON FACEBOOK AND TWITTER
JOIN THE MOON PHOTO GROUP ON FLICKR

MAP SYMBOLS

▦▦▦ Expressway	◖ Highlight	✗ Airfield	⚓ Golf Course
——— Primary Road	○ City/Town	✈ Airport	🅿 Parking Area
⋯⋯ Secondary Road	◉ State Capital	▲ Mountain	◣ Archaeological Site
▪ ▪ ▪ Unpaved Road	⊛ National Capital	✦ Unique Natural Feature	⛪ Church
- - - - Trail	★ Point of Interest		
⋯⋯⋯ Ferry	• Accommodation	🦋 Waterfall	⛽ Gas Station
- -- - Railroad	▾ Restaurant/Bar	♠ Park	◌ Glacier
▦▦ Pedestrian Walkway	■ Other Location	▣ Trailhead	◫ Mangrove
⫻⫻⫻ Stairs	△ Campground	🎿 Skiing Area	▨ Reef
			▨ Swamp

CONVERSION TABLES

°C = (°F – 32) / 1.8
°F = (°C x 1.8) + 32
1 inch = 2.54 centimeters (cm)
1 foot = 0.304 meters (m)
1 yard = 0.914 meters
1 mile = 1.6093 kilometers (km)
1 km = 0.6214 miles
1 fathom = 1.8288 m
1 chain = 20.1168 m
1 furlong = 201.168 m
1 acre = 0.4047 hectares
1 sq km = 100 hectares
1 sq mile = 2.59 square km
1 ounce = 28.35 grams
1 pound = 0.4536 kilograms
1 short ton = 0.90718 metric ton
1 short ton = 2,000 pounds
1 long ton = 1.016 metric tons
1 long ton = 2,240 pounds
1 metric ton = 1,000 kilograms
1 quart = 0.94635 liters
1 US gallon = 3.7854 liters
1 Imperial gallon = 4.5459 liters
1 nautical mile = 1.852 km

°FAHRENHEIT °CELSIUS

230 — — 110
220 — — 100 WATER BOILS
210 —
200 — — 90
190 —
180 — — 80
170 —
160 — — 70
150 —
140 — — 60
130 —
120 — — 50
110 —
100 — — 40
90 — — 30
80 —
70 — — 20
60 —
50 — — 10
40 —
30 — — 0 WATER FREEZES
20 —
10 — — -10
0 —
-10 — — -20
-20 — — -30
-30 —
-40 — — -40

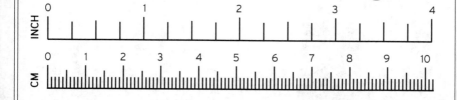

INCH 0 1 2 3 4

CM 0 1 2 3 4 5 6 7 8 9 10

MOON SPOTLIGHT LOUISVILLE & THE BOURBON TRAIL

Avalon Travel
a member of the Perseus Books Group
1700 Fourth Street
Berkeley, CA 94710, USA
www.moon.com

Editor and Series Manager: Kathryn Ettinger
Copy Editor: Ellie Winters
Graphics and Production Coordinator:
    Lucie Ericksen
Cover Designer: Kathryn Osgood
Map Editor: Brice Ticen
Cartographers: Lohnes & Wright, Kat Bennett

ISBN: 978-1-61238-045-2

Front cover photo: barn in a Kentucky field © Laurin Rinder | Dreamstime.com

Title page photo: Louisville skyline © dndavis/123 RF

Printed in the United States

ABOUT THE AUTHOR

Theresa Dowell Blackinton

Theresa Dowell Blackinton was born and raised in Louisville, Kentucky, and spent her childhood visiting the state's attractions with her parents and three brothers. She left Kentucky to attend college at Rice University in Houston, Texas, and has been on the move ever since – living in Freiburg, Germany; Athens, Greece; Washington DC; and Durham, North Carolina; and spending time in more than 50 countries. But she still considers the Bluegrass State home.

While researching this book, Theresa was reminded of her home state's interesting history and awesome natural beauty – but what she most enjoyed was getting to interact with Kentucky's warm and welcoming people, all of whom had interesting stories to tell.

Theresa is also the author of *Moon Take a Hike Washington DC* and has written for multiple newspapers and magazines. She provides updated information about Kentucky travel at www.bluegrasstraveler.com.